Mami No Estaba Mintiendo

(Mom wasn't lying)

by:

Carla Hernandez

Copyright

Copyright © [2025] by [Carla Hernandez]

All rights reserved.

No portion of this book may be reproduced in any form without written permission from the publisher or author, except as permitted by U.S. copyright law.

TABLE OF CONTENTS

INTRODUCTION

ABOUT AUTHOR

DEDICATION

CHAPTER 1-THE MOMENT THEY STOPPED LISTENING

CHAPTER2-THEY BELIEVED THEM….

CHAPTER3-RULES, RISKS, REALITY

CHAPTER4-KIDS LOVE OUTSIDE OPINIONS…

CHAPTER5-HOW TO BE THE PARENT THEY DENY BUT…

CHAPTER6-WHEN GENTLE PARENTING ISN'T ENOUGH

CHAPTER7-THE APOLOGIES COME LATER

CHAPTER8-THE ART OF SAYING NOTHING AND ….

CHAPTER9-WHEN YOU STOP SAVING THEM, THEY….

CHAPTER10-WHEN I HAD TO ADMIT I WAS WRONG

CHAPTER 11 - WHAT MY DENIAL ALMOST COST ME

CHAPTER 12 - BOUNDARIES: BEGINNER'S GUIDE…

CHAPTER 13 - THE PARENT YOU NEEDED VS THE ….

CHAPTER 14 - RAISING LEADERS, NOT ….

CHAPTER 15 - LET ME THROW THIS IN HERE

CHAPTER 16 - OH, ALSO…

CHAPTER 17 - GOD EDUCATES JUST NOT THE WAY….

CHAPTER 18 - THE RESPECT THEY SWORE THEY…

CHAPTER 19 - THE CHILD YOU WERE VS THE PARENT….

CHAPTER 20 - MOM NEVER LIED, YOU JUST NEVER…

CHAPTER 21 - YOU JUST AIN'T $100 BILL TO BE…

CHAPTER 22 - OUR LEGACY STARTS WHERE THE…

CHAPTER 23 - GENERATIONAL CURSES VS….

CHAPTER 24 - RAISING KIDS IN A DIGITAL….

CHAPTER 25 - WHEN YOUR CHILD HAS A…

BONUS CHAPTER 1- WHEN THE OTHER PARENT…

BONUS CHAPTER 2-HOW KIDS PLAY ONE PARENT….

AUTHORS NOTE

BEFORE YOU CLOSE THIS BOOK

ABOUT THE AUTHOR

Carla Hernandez, also known as Queen of Hustle, is a powerhouse of resilience, purpose, and divine alignment. A single mother of three

who rebuilt her life from the ashes emotionally, spiritually, financially, and generationally. She stands as living proof that broken beginnings

can still create powerful destinies. Born into chaos but raised by faith, strategy, and grit, She's transformed every wound into wisdom,

embodies the duality of spiritual depth and scientific knowledge, blending neuroscience, psychology, and biblical principles to teach families

how to rebuild themselves from the inside out. Her voice is both poetic and street-smart, balancing truth with tenderness, humor with holiness,

and discipline with deep compassion. Carla is not just an author, she is an entrepreneur, healer, coach, musician, educator, and legacy architect.

She builds entire worlds for her children and her community, proving that guidance doesn't require perfection….

Just courage, honesty, and consistency.

Her life demanded leadership long before she understood her own power. After losing the fathers of her children, she carried her family alone

no shortcuts, no excuses. Relying only on faith, resilience, and her relentless determination to end generational cycles once and for all. Today,

Carla helps parents and teens step into emotional maturity, self-control, and spiritual stability through her writing, coaching, and education

systems. Her work stands at the intersection of personal transformation and family restoration, bold, raw, culturally rich, and deeply healing.

She believes this truth with her whole soul: "What you didn't receive becomes what you are destined to give." With every chapter she writes and

every life she touches, Carla continues to raise leaders, heal homes, awaken faith, and prove that alignment is not a moment, it is a lifestyle.

Teenagers swear they understand the world..until the world teaches them a lesson they never saw coming. Parents try to guide them..until they realize talking is no match for the generation that "knows better." This book is where both sides finally meet. As a mother of three teens,

I learned that raising kids today requires more than lectures, warnings, or old-school "because I said so" / occasional whooping. Kids are growing

up in a world where attention becomes identity, common sense feels rare, and validation from strangers weighs more than wisdom from home.

And yet… Not every child has a mother or parent who teaches, protects, or even tries. Not every home feels safe. Not every parent knows *how*

to parent. Some kids raise themselves while adults around them fall asleep at the wheel. This book exists for all of them. For the parents who care

but feel unheard. For the teens who think they know life but haven't lived enough of it.

For the youth who didn't get a present parent and still want to break the cycle. For the families who want healing without fear, pressure, or silence.

Inside these pages, you'll find neuroscience explained simply…. why teens reject advice, why they chase outside approval, and how their developing brain confuses independence with recklessness. Biblical truth that grounds every chapter, not religion, but relationship, real-life stories that teach

what lectures can't. Tools for self-control, discipline, and emotional maturity strategies parents can use today that actually work.

Actions, not arguments, that shift a home's dynamic prayers that restore peace and protection wisdom from God, psychology, and lived experience

I'm not a perfect parent. I've made mistakes. I didn't get a guidebook either. But I learned that you can write your own and make sure someone else

doesn't have to struggle the same way. It's a reminder that success doesn't require evil, shortcuts, rebellion, or chaos. Success can come from clarity,

structure, faith, and connection with God because, **God gives wisdom to those who seek him**, and once you've tasted his guidance, you'll never

want to let go. Whether you're a parent, a teen, or someone trying to break the chains of the past, this book will help you see clearly:

life's lessons hit softer when you learn them early. And healing begins the moment you decide the cycle stops with you.

INTRODUCTION

THE MOMENT I REALIZED TALKING WASN'T ENOUGH"

There comes a point in every mother's life where you look at your child not the baby you rocked, not the toddler who followed you everywhere

but the teenager standing in front of you with a chest full of opinions and a mind half-built but fully convinced…and you realize: "Okay…

Talking ain't working anymore." Not because they're bad kids. Not because they don't love you. Or because you failed.   But because somewhere

between childhood and adulthood, between hormones and identity, between TikTok psychology and real-world consequences,

they start believing the biggest lie of that age:

"I know what I'm doing."   And as a mother, you watch them confidently walk toward a wall you've already hit a thousand times.   You try to warn them, they roll their eyes. You try again, they think you're dramatic. You raise your voice and now you're the villain. Then…you go silent.

Not because you gave up, but because you woke up. You finally understand something that parenting books never tell you:

Kids don't learn from our lectures, they learn from our actions and our consistency. They learn from life. And sometimes…life has to speak louder

than you. This book wasn't born out of frustration. It was born out of clarity. The moment I realized my words were bouncing off teenage armor,

I decided to show, not tell. To lead, not chase. To guide, not beg. And yes, I wrote this entire book as a living lesson. Because my kids, like most

teenagers today, don't understand the world yet.

They're smart, but not seasoned. They're bold, but not built. They think they know, but they don't even know what they don't know.

And that's okay, It's normal, It's biology.

The brain that controls logic, danger, and foresight the prefrontal cortex is the LAST thing to mature. Science proves it. God already warned us.

And mothers feel it daily. Teenagers chase approval from strangers, but question the wisdom of the woman who would die for them. They forget

that the world outside doesn't love them. The world outside doesn't protect them. The world outside will happily teach them lessons…..

harshly without mercy. Truth no one says out loud: comfort is not preparation. Soft parenting fails where discipline is required. Words matter less

than actions. A good example teaches more than indulgence ever will.. Not every child gets a mother like mine.

Not every child gets a mother like me. And not every parent knows how to parent. Some kids raise themselves. Some are emotionally orphaned.

Others want guidance but don't know how to ask. Some parents try, but don't know how to communicate. Some parents were never taught love,

safety, or patience. So how do we break the chains when the chains raised us?

Through faith, discipline, action. Through understanding the brain God designed, and humility. Through repetition and connection. And through

books like this one. I'm not a perfect mother. I've failed, cried, screamed, learned, apologized, and grown. But I decided to stop surviving my

motherhood and start understanding it. I decided to stop parenting through fear, through passed learnings that were the least insightful at best,

and start parenting through wisdom. And that wisdom didn't come from YouTube, or Google. Or some Instagram influencer.

It came from the only source who has never failed me: God. Not religion. Not tradition. Not performance. Just Him. The God who says,

"Seek and you shall find." The God who gives wisdom freely to those who ask. The God who turned my chaos into clarity, my exhaustion into

discipline and my pain into purpose.

My children don't need a perfect mother, they need a connected one, Connected to truth, to self-control, to neuroscience, to boundaries, to purpose, to patience, to accountability….to God.

This book is that connection.

It's part science because the brain matters.

It's part psychology because behavior matters.

It's part spirituality because God matters.

It's part storytelling because experiences matter.

It's part honesty because healing requires truth.

And its part instruction because families need guidance.

This book is for:

the parent who is tired of repeating themselves

the teen who thinks they're ready for the world

the child who grew up without guidance

the young parent trying to do better

the cycle-breaker

the mother at her limit

the father who wants to understand

the kid who wants to grow

the family ready to evolve together

This book is for the whole house. Because when one person grows, everyone grows. When one person learns self-control, When one person

breaks the cycle, the generations behind them breathe easier. And when a family puts God in the center, everything comes into alignment.

Slowly, painfully sometimes, but faithfully. I wrote this book as a parent, as a daughter, as a woman rebuilding from trauma. I wrote this book as a

mother raising teenagers in a generation hungry for guidance. And I wrote this book as someone who finally realized: We weren't born with a

guidebook but nothing stops us from writing our own and leaving it behind for someone else. This is mine. This is yours now. Use it well.

DEDICATION

For my three children, mi corazón dividido en tres cuerpos. *The ones God trusted me with when life stole what should've been yours.*

who lost their fathers too young, who had to learn strength before childhood was done, who watched me stand alone in places where two parents were

meant to stand. I know what you've carried. I know what you've missed. And I know the weight I've had to lift to become both mother and father

in a world that never goes easy on the parent who stays. You are the reason I wake up fighting, the reason I learned discipline,

faith, tenderness, and grit. You are the chapters I didn't know how to write until I lived them.

Thank you for forgiving my imperfections, for growing with me while I healed, and for teaching me that love doesn't need perfection to be powerful.

Everything I build, I build for you. Every lesson, every truth, every warning, every prayer was born from the days I had no choice but to keep going even when grief tried to bury me too. You three are the reason I survived. The reason I rebuilt. The reason I learned how to stand without

collapsing. You are why I fought through tears, worked through exhaustion, and prayed through pain.

This book exists because I refused to let our story end at loss. I refused to let the absence of fathers become the absence of guidance. I refused to let

grief raise you, so I raised you myself, flawed, tired, but never abandoning my post. To every child reading this who grew up without a present parent,

may you find direction here. To every mother raising warriors alone whether by choice, by tragedy, or by the failure of others, may you feel seen in

these pages. This book is an offering to your resilience. Your tears are prayers. Your discipline is legacy. Your sacrifices are seeds. And one day,

your children will understand the weight you carried and the strength it took to keep going.

And above all *for God,* the One who filled the empty spaces, held me when no one else did, carried what I couldn't, and taught me that being alone doesn't mean being abandoned.   The one who turned my wounds into wisdom, my fear into fire, and my motherhood into ministry.   Every page of this

book exists because you refused to let me break even when life tried to shatter me.

This is my offering, my testimony, my legacy for you, my children, and for everyone who still believes that love, discipline, and faith

can rebuild a future from the ashes of what was lost.

To the parents who never had guidance themselves thank you for choosing to rise instead of repeat.

For choosing healing over habit.

For choosing growth over generational silence.

For choosing to be the mother or father you needed as a child.

To the readers, thank you for trusting me with your heart.   For opening these pages while carrying your own story, your own battles, your own

broken places.   May these words meet you where you are and lift you where you're going.

To every person who ever doubted me, betrayed me, left me, or tried to dim my light, Thank You. Your absence became my discipline.

Your silence became my strength. Your rejection became God's redirection.

And finally…

to the girl I used to be the scared one, the hurting one, the quiet one, the one who prayed with tears instead of words thank you for surviving long

enough for me to write this book. I am who I am because you refused to quit on days no one even knew you were fighting.

This is not the end. This my reminder that even in the darkest seasons…

Dios siempre está obrando (God is always working in your life)

Chapter 1

THE MOMENT THEY STOPPED LISTENING

I'm standing in the kitchen, talking to a teenager whose face I have loved since the day God placed her in my arms… and I can tell by the way she's

blinking that I just lost her. Not because I'm wrong, or that she don't care. But because her mind has slipped into that teenage portal where adults

become background noise.

You know the look, eyes glaze over just enough, shoulders shift, breathing changes.   Their spirit slides into a stance that says: "I hear you…

but I already decided you're overreacting." And something inside me…something ancient, wise, exhausted, and fed up rises. Because this isn't my

first child. This isn't my first teenager. This isn't my first battle with the illusion of "I know everything." After you've raised multiple kids alone, after burying the men who were supposed to help raise them… you learn to read teenagers the way sailors read the ocean. The sky changes,

the air shifts, and before the storm hits, you know.

So I pause mid-sentence. I breathe. I look at this child.. my child…and I realize: "Talking won't work here." Not today!

Not in this stage of life, with the brain they currently have and the world they're growing up in. The world tells them they're grown.

Social media tells them they're wise. Their friends tell them they're right. And their brain tells them they're invincible.

A dangerous combo. I am the only one telling them the truth. But truth, spoken to a teenager at the wrong moment, can sound like an attack.

So instead of yelling, lecturing, instead of repeating myself like a broken record, I do the thing most parents fear: I stop talking. Not out of defeat

out of strategy.

Because silence is a teacher too. Life speaks louder than a mother's frustration. Kids today don't trust words, they trust results. And in this moment,

I understand the assignment:

It's time to show them, not tell them. You can't force understanding, you can't force maturity. You can't force wisdom onto a brain that's not

finished cooking. But!... you *can* lay foundations. You *can* set boundaries, demonstrate consequences. You *can* show what calm looks like.

By modeling discipline, self-respect, and faith. You *can* act in a way that leaves a permanent imprint long after the noise fades. I understand for some

parents a butt whooping may help, but to what extent? What is being avoided by giving the whooping?

Kids need limits they can't negotiate away

Consequences must hurt *enough* to matter (not physically)

Parents must be willing to be disliked

Love without authority creates chaos

Authority without love creates fear

Sometimes you don't need raised hands. You need an unmovable spine.   No one is born with an unmovable spine.   It's built.   It's the moment you
choose long-term outcomes over short-term peace,
most firm parents weren't always firm.   They tried explaining, negotiating, rescuing.
They watched it backfire.   Pain is a brutal but effective teacher.   You practice calm enforcement. Not yelling. Not hitting.

Just: *This is the rule.   This is the consequence.   I will follow through every time.*   Consistency builds authority faster than force ever did.
You accept discomfort as part of the job.   Guilt. Anger. Silence. Tears. Pushback.   You stop treating those as emergencies and start
treating them as *weather*.

That's the spine:
Not rage.
Not fear.
Not dominance.
But resolve

And here's the quiet truth: People who rely on force often don't trust themselves to hold that resolve without it.

I remember my mom telling me "Raise them the way I raise you. With consistency. With truth. With love that doesn't bend."

So I stand there in that kitchen, in my imperfect house, with my imperfect children, living my imperfect life and I decide:

"This moment right here… this is where the book begins."

Because if my kids won't listen to my voice today, they WILL hear my voice in these pages tomorrow. And if they don't understand life now,

these words will follow them into adulthood, ready to wake them at the exact moment they need it.

I had to survive to learn. But my children, your children, the children reading this deserve better. They deserve a mother (or a mentor) whose honesty is louder than the world's lies. They deserve a blueprint. They deserve wisdom before wounds. They deserve warnings before scars.

They deserve a chance at life without learning everything the hard way.

So Chapter One begins with the truth: Teenagers stop listening long before they stop needing guidance. And the moment they tune you out

is the moment you start teaching differently. This book is that difference.

Teach them the way they should go,

and even when they grow older,

they will not depart from it."

PROVERBS *22:6*

A reminder that guidance given in truth will echo long after the noise fades.

NEUROSCIENCE INSIGHT:

THE TEENAGE BRAIN: WHY THEY "KNOW EVERYTHING"

The prefrontal cortex (the part responsible for logic, judgment, and self-control) is *still under construction* until age 25.

Teens rely heavily on the amygdala, the emotional center, which exaggerates risk-taking and defensiveness.

Their brain prioritizes peer approval over parental wisdom this is biologically normal, not rebellion.

They hear correction as an attack, not protection.

Their internal world feels louder and more intense than reality.

Translation:

Your child isn't hard-headed by choice, their brain is literally rewiring itself.

This book teaches them how to master the storm instead of being steered by it.

THE REBUTTAL

What someone doubtful would say

"Okay but… isn't all this a little dramatic? You're acting like teenagers are impossible, like they're these mysterious creatures

nobody knows how to talk to.

Kids have ALWAYS rolled their eyes. Teens have ALWAYS thought they knew everything. Why act like it's different now?   Why all this talk about

brains still cooking and silence being a strategy and God whispered guidance?

Isn't it your job as the parent to just TALK/YELL/SPANK until they understand? Why do you make it seem like they're neurologically

unable to listen? Aren't you overthinking it? Aren't you giving teenagers excuses? Why can't they just listen like we did?"

THE ANSWER

I'm not being dramatic. I'm being accurate.   You're confusing **disrespect** with development.   And confusing rebellion with biology.

You're confusing your childhood with their world.

We didn't grow up with: social media validating immaturity, overstimulation every second, screens hijacking dopamine peer pressure 24/7.

These kids have access to EVERYTHING and understanding of NOTHING.

This generation's brain isn't the brain you and I had. And yes, it is my job as a parent to teach them…. But teaching doesn't mean screaming into

a storm hoping the wind suddenly respects you. Whooping them with brooms and breaking plates on our heads, the way they used to do to us.

Teaching is understanding the wiring behind the behavior.

Teaching is adjusting your method not your message.

Teaching is knowing when talking becomes noise and silence becomes strategy.

Teaching is raising them, Not always with explanations, but always with consistency.

So no,

I'm not giving teens excuses. I'm giving parents INFORMATION. Because once you know *how* the teenage mind works, you stop fighting the child

and start guiding the brain. And THAT…. is when transformation finally begins."

Chapter 2

THEY BELIEVE THEM BEFORE THEY BELIEVE YOU

There's a moment every parent knows too well: You say something. They don't listen. A stranger says the exact same thing… and suddenly your

kid thinks it's gospel. You could scream. You could cry. You could ask God why he entrusted you with these creatures. But then you breathe and

remember: This is normal. Annoying. Infuriating. But normal.

I'm watching one of my kids sit on the edge of the couch, scrolling, snorting, laughing at some influencer who just said the SAME darn thing I've

been preaching since they were in diapers. They look at me with that "Mami, did you know this?" face. And inside my soul, something unclenches…

not because I'm calm, but because I'm learning. I don't need to win the moment. I need to win the war. I don't need credit. I need clarity.

So instead of saying, "I told you that already" I say: "Good. You needed to hear it." Because the truth is… I don't care who gets the credit

as long as my child gets the lesson. As a mother I learned the hard way that motherhood isn't about pride, It's about protection. If your child needs to

hear wisdom from a coach, a pastor, a teacher, a friend, a stranger so be it. Let their brain latch onto whoever delivers the message cleanest.

I am not in competition with the world. I am in collaboration with their future.

All roads of wisdom eventually lead back home. When the world hurts them, they run to me. When life confuses them, they look for me. Because

I'm the one that shown up. When adults outside disappoint them, they come sit in my room. When they hear the truth elsewhere, they remember

my voice. They may not understand that now, but one day they will.

One day they will see that every outsider they trusted was just echoing what their mother had been saying all along.

Kids with good homes still look for outside proof that their mother or father or mentor isn't exaggerating. And kids without stable homes?

They cling to any voice that feels steady. But sooner or later every child learns this: A mother's warnings aren't criticism. They are prophecy.

Not because we're perfect. Not because we know everything. But because we've lived enough to recognize danger in the dark.

This chapter is not about controlling your child. It's about understanding their psychology so they don't become a casualty of their own blind spots.

Let the outsider speak. Let the mentor validate. Let the world teach lightly so you don't have to teach painfully. Your voice is the root.

Theirs are the branches. Both are needed. One day your child will realize you weren't trying to restrict their life you were trying to save it.

The wise listen and add to their learning………..but fools despise instruction."

PROVERBS 1:5–7

A reminder that wisdom is not about age, it's about humility.

SIDEBAR FOR TEENS

Hey, you. Yeah… you. Here's what nobody tells you:

Your brain is still building the part that makes smart decisions. It's not your fault.. it's biology. But it is YOUR responsibility.

Your parent isn't trying to ruin your fun. They're trying to save you from the pain they've already lived through. You don't have to agree.

But you do need to think.

Here's your challenge:

Before you react, ask yourself: "Am I rejecting this because it's wrong…

or because I don't want to hear it?"

If it's the second one,

you just discovered your first sign of maturity:

self-control. Keep going. You're building a future, not an ego.

REFLECTION QUESTIONS:

For Parents:

When was the last time your teen believed someone else over you?

Did you react emotionally or strategically? What message matters more the wisdom or the credit?

What outsider voices can your partner do with you to reinforce your teachings?

For Teens / Tweens / Kids:

Who do you listen to most and why?

Do you dismiss your parent because they're "wrong" or because they're familiar?

What advice have you heard from multiple people lately?

What is one thing you can try listening to without arguing?

PARENTS PRAYER FOR THIS CHAPTER

Dear God, Give me the humility to speak wisely and the patience to guide gently.

Help my child recognize truth no matter who delivers it. Strengthen our communication,

our trust, and our connection. Protect their mind from confusion, their heart from deception,

and their steps from danger Let Your voice be the loudest in this home.

Amen.

TEENS / TWEEN / KIDS PRAYER FOR THIS CHAPTER

God,
help me shut up long enough to listen.
I don't know everything, even when I think I do.

Help me stop brushing off correction
just because it annoys me
or hurts my pride.

Teach me why wisdom matters
before I mess things up bad enough
that I can't undo it.

Help me respect the people
trying to guide me,
even when I don't like what they're saying.

Give me judgment, not just confidence.
Fear of You, not fear of missing out.

I want knowledge that keeps me alive,
not lessons I have to learn the hard way.

Amen.

NEUROSCIENCE INSIGHT

WHY TEENS BELIEVE STRANGERS BEFORE BELIEVING YOU

Adolescents experience heightened reward activation in the brain when validated by peers or "outsiders."

Social approval triggers dopamine in teens stronger than parental approval.

Teens interpret parental guidance as control, but interpret outsider feedback as respect.

This isn't disloyalty, it's neurological wiring.

When the parental voice sounds "familiar," teens tune it out. Outsiders sound "new," so their brain pays attention.

Translation: Your kid isn't choosing strangers over you their brain is programmed to seek "outside confirmation"

as part of identity formation.

This chapter teaches how to use this understanding strategically instead of emotionally

THE REBUTTAL

Overthinking a bit?

"Pero ven acá…Hold up a second

Isn't this just… overthinking? Kids have listened to their parents for generations.   And have ignored them in the same sense…

Teenagers have always been dramatic.   This is normal human behavior.   Why turn it into neuroscience?

Why act like their brain is some fragile project?   You keep saying 'their brain,' 'their development,' 'their psychology.'

But aren't you just giving them a pass?

What happened to the old days where one look from your mother was enough?   Why not just discipline them more?   Take the phone.

Ground them. Yell louder. Explain the consequences until they finally get it.

Why do parents today need strategies? Silence? Patience? Collaboration with outside voices? Isn't that just letting the world raise your kid?

Aren't you worried you're doing too much? Or not enough? Or making excuses for behavior that needs correction?"

THE ANSWER

I've heard this argument my whole life.   Hear me out, Corazon. I'm not giving teenagers excuses.

You're confusing what worked in YOUR childhood with a world that no longer exists.

You say, 'Just yell.'   But yelling doesn't rewire a brain. It just scares a child into silence.

You say, 'Just take their phone.'   But consequences without connection teach fear, not wisdom.

You say, 'Just discipline harder.'   But discipline without understanding creates rebellion, not transformation.

You say it's 'normal.'   But you're calling trauma 'tradition,' and fear 'obedience.'

And I'm not raising kids who obey out of fear. I'm raising kids who understand. Who think. Who reason. Who make choices from clarity,

not pressure.   Who grow into leaders, not followers.

You think I'm collaborating with outsiders because I'm weak. No. I'm collaborating with whatever tool God gives me. because I'm STRATEGIC.

If my child won't hear truth from me today, but will from a coach, a mentor, a pastor, a stranger, why would I block the blessing?

Wisdom is wisdom no matter whose mouth it comes from.

I'm guiding them toward destiny.

You want obedience.

I want transformation, and transformation requires understanding the brain, the child, the world they're growing in, and the

God who entrusted them to me.

So no…..

I'm not doing too much. I'm doing exactly what this generation needs.

So when someone says, *"Isn't that just letting the world raise your kid?"* is said by people who hand their kids to:

a government system, rotating adults with 30+ students, peers who are also still figuring life out with screens, trends, and algorithms for
7-8 hours a day.

That *is* letting the world help raise them, If parents don't establish:

Authority
Values
Discipline
Discernment

Then the loudest voices win.   And in school, those voices are usually other kids, not adults.

The honest answer is:

School can teach **information**.   It does not teach **wisdom**.   It does not teach **judgment**.   It does not teach **character**.
That's supposed to come from home.

The world is already involved.   My job is to make sure my child is trained enough, not to be shaped by it.

Parents who don't prepare their kids for reality aren't protecting them they're outsourcing the lesson to consequences..

Let's talk about this for real.

Parents send their kids to school because, in the eyes of the law and society, parents are expected to work nonstop just to survive. To make money.
To pay bills. To keep up. Somewhere along the way, actually **raising** our children got outsourced because we're told this is the "right" way to live.

Then people say, *"It's hard to run a business."* But somehow it's not hard to scroll social media for hours.
Not hard to binge shows.
Not hard to stay distracted.

Yet suddenly it's "too hard" to pick up a book, listen to a podcast, seek guidance, go to a library, or do real due diligence on how wealthy people
actually think, learn, and move. That old excuse *"I have to work to make money and pay my bills"*….yes, it's real… but it's also **small thinking**
when it becomes the reason you never evolve.

Then the same parents complain: "My kid doesn't listen." "Where did they learn those words?" "Why do they have this attitude?"

Ask yourself….who raised them? What system shaped them? What example did they watch every day?

You're following the rules of a broken system designed to keep you exhausted, distracted, and dependent. Think about it.

Even me, as a single mother, I found a way. I work from home. I homeschool my kids. I'm building a business.

And no, it wasn't easy. I had to move from state to state just to find something affordable. Somewhere I could actually breathe. Family?

People love to ask, *"Where's your family?"* But what is family for, if they're never there when you need support? Mine didn't help me.

Not financially. Not emotionally. Not logistically.

So I did what I had to do.

I took the step many people are afraid to take. I moved somewhere new where no one knew me. No safety net. No familiar faces. Just vision, faith, and responsibility. I rebuilt from scratch. I learned skills at home….FOR FREE. I studied….FOR

FREE while raising my kids.
I adjusted, adapted, and refused to stay stuck.

Information is everywhere. IT'S FREE. But only if you're willing to look beyond comfort and excuses. At one point in time…I didn't know
where to start, what dot do, or who to go to… The only one who was able to help me was God when I prayed to knowledge and guidance.
He gave me that and more.

So the real question is this: Are you up for the challenge of changing your life? Or would you rather stay where you are…complaining you don't
spend enough time with your kids, while barely knowing who they're becoming? Complaining you don't know how?…

Because freedom isn't easy. But neither is regret.

Chapter 3

RULES, RISKS AND REALITY

There's a dangerous myth parents whisper to themselves: "If I give them love, safety, food, stability, respect…they'll listen."
And you find out real quick loving your kid does not guarantee compliance.

I'm watching one of mine walk across the living room, comfortable, fed, safe, warm, but carrying an attitude like the world owes them something.

And I get it. I created that comfort. I built a home where they could breathe, laugh, sleep without fear, grow without chaos, and heal without hiding.

But comfort is a double-edged sword. Because when a child has never truly felt desperation, they think warnings are exaggerations.

When a child has never been abandoned, they think advice is control. When a child has never seen evil up close,
they assume the world is kinder than it is.

They're not ungrateful, they're inexperienced. And experience is the fastest, cruelest, most unforgettable teacher.

So I look at my child today, and I remind myself: "They're not always misbehaving. They're learning."

Kids in good homes still rebel.

Kids with present parents still test limits.

Kids who have structure still push against walls just to measure their own strength.

I don't take it personally anymore. Because I understand something deeper now, something I wish I had known when I first became a mother:

A child who feels safe enough to challenge you is still safer than the child who learned silence as survival.

And yes, it hurts when they roll their eyes. Yes, it stings when they dismiss your warnings. Yes, it's frustrating when they act like life is a game you only *think* you understand.

But I remind myself:

They don't know grief the way I do.

They don't know loss the way I do.

They don't know danger the way I do.

They don't know trauma the way I do.

Thank God.

The fact that my children don't fear what I fear means I succeeded at something.

But now I have a new job: turn their comfort into character.   Turn their safety into strength.   Turn their stability into wisdom.

Not by removing the comfort but by teaching them responsibility inside of it.

Because comfort without humility creates entitlement. And entitlement is the graveyard of good futures.

But comfort with guidance?

Comfort with boundaries?

Comfort with accountability?

That creates leaders.

So yes, kids from good homes still don't listen sometimes. Not because you failed. Because their brain is growing, their identity is forming, their ego is experimenting, and their spirit is stretching.

Your job as a parent is not to break your child's spirit..it's to shape it.

(The military breaks down recruits to rebuild them for a specific mission, forcing them to unlearn old habits and adopt new ones.)

Parenting isn't about obedience to an institution; it's about building judgment, resilience, and character so your child can thrive in the real world.

The goal is formation, not destruction."

They may not listen today, but they will remember tomorrow. And the day life hits them hard, your voice will echo louder than every influencer,

every friend, every stranger they once trusted more.

A good home with guidance and faith doesn't guarantee perfect kids.

In short, a good home guarantees preparation, not perfection. It doesn't control outcomes, but it equips your kids so the outcomes don't destroy them.

"A wise child brings joy, but a foolish one brings grief."

PROVERBS 10:1

A reminder that choices echo deeper than intentions.

PRAYER FOR THIS CHAPTER

Dear God,

Thank You for the stability You've allowed me to build.

Help my child see the blessings around them.

Grant them humility, wisdom, and clarity.

Teach them to value safety, structure, and guidance.

Help me parent with love, patience, and strength.

Protect their mind from entitlement

and their heart from pride.

Guide this home with Your truth.

Amen.

TEEN / TWEEN / KIDS PRAYER:

God,
help me see what's right even when it's hard.
Help me listen when I don't want to.
Give me wisdom to make good choices, not just the easy ones.
Help me respect the people trying to guide me, even when I don't like it.
Keep me humble, teach me patience, and protect me from pride and entitlement.
Let me see the value in rules, structure, and guidance..not as walls, but as tools to help me survive and grow.
Amen.

NEUROSCIENCE INSIGHT:

WHY GOOD HOMES DON'T GUARANTEE COOPERATIVE KIDS

The reward system in teen brains is hypersensitive, they chase excitement even when they have stability.

Kids raised in healthy homes often take safety for granted, assuming risk has no real consequences.

The absence of chaos makes them believe the world is "soft."

Their brain is wired to test boundaries, because testing = identity formation.

Teens raised with love often assume love will always protect them, even from themselves.

Translation:

A good home doesn't make them obedient.

It makes them *comfortable* and comfort creates blind spots.

This chapter teaches how to turn comfort into wisdom, not complacency.

SIDEBAR FOR TEEN/TWEENS:

You don't realize it yet, but growing up in a stable home is a blessing people beg God for.

Safety isn't weakness. Rules aren't punishment. Boundaries aren't control.   They are love in disguise, for ones self and to others

You don't have to agree with every rule.   But at least respect the fact that someone cares enough to guide you.

Here's your challenge:

Before you break a rule, ask:

"Am I doing this because it's smart…
or because I want to feel grown for five seconds?"

If it's the second one

slow down.

You're building a life,

not a moment.

REFLECTION QUESTIONS

<u>For Parents:</u>

What comforts have your kids taken for granted?

How can you turn comfort into character-building?

Are your reactions driven by ego or purpose?

What lesson can be taught through action instead of words?

<u>For Teens:</u>

What do you have that other teens might wish for?

Do you mistake comfort for invincibility?

What rule do you break just because it "feels grown"?

How can you show maturity this week without rebellion?

THE REBUTTAL

"Okay, I get what you're saying, but this feels like a lot of assumptions wrapped up in a very heavy-handed worldview.   First, you keep talking about

kids from good homes being 'inexperienced' or 'blind' because they haven't faced danger or desperation but isn't that just part of growing up?

Kids will make mistakes. They will experience pain.

Trying to frame every misstep as a lack of preparation risks over-analyzing normal behavior.   Teens push boundaries because that's literally how

they learn to be independent humans, not because they're spoiled or ungrateful.   You talk about 'turning comfort into character' and suggest that kids

are testing limits as a way of measuring strength but this reads a lot like controlling their every choice under the guise of shaping them.

Isn't there a difference between guidance and constant monitoring?   Between teaching accountability and making every mistake a moral lesson?

Kids need autonomy to develop judgment on their own. You say parenting isn't about obedience to an institution but when you frame it this way,

it almost is: structure, rules, boundaries, accountability, constant shaping. That can feel like a kind of subtle imprisonment, not freedom.

You mention neuroscience and the teen brain's reward system, saying that comfort creates blind spots and makes teens assume the world is soft.

But aren't you oversimplifying? Yes, teen brains are reward-sensitive but that doesn't automatically mean stability creates entitlement.

Many teens raised in structured homes are thoughtful, humble, and capable of empathy.

Painting comfort as inherently dangerous risks creating unnecessary guilt or anxiety in both parents and kids. And the faith angle the emphasis on

teaching kids humility, wisdom, and respect for guidance is valid, but it also reads like you're assuming that the only way to internalize values

is through strict structure and constant correction. Isn't modeling faith, curiosity, and critical thinking just as important as enforcing obedience?

Some of the strongest kids I know learned how to make moral choices because they were trusted, not because they were constantly shaped inside a

controlled environment. Even the teen-side advice comes off as prescriptive: 'Before you break a rule, ask if it's smart or just to feel grown.'

But isn't part of growing up learning to take calculated risks, make mistakes, and feel the consequences? Framing all rule-breaking as immature or

ego-driven risks treating normal independence and experimentation as rebellion to be corrected. Teens need some space to fail and learn on

their own terms. Finally, there's the repeated framing of life as harsh and unforgiving, as if every teen who doesn't absorb your lessons will inevitably

suffer permanent consequences. That's fear-based.

Kids can and do survive mistakes, even in 'good homes,' and some of the lessons they learn outside of structured guidance are just as valuable as the

ones inside it. By emphasizing control and shaping over autonomy, you risk making comfort feel conditional, even though you rightly say comfort is a blessing. In short, your chapter reads like a manifesto of preparation and control, and while it's well-intentioned, it risks underestimating the

importance of independence, self-directed learning, and the normal, messy process of growing up. Not every moment of rebellion is a failure of

preparation, and not every teen mistake is a consequence that only strict guidance could prevent. The world will teach lessons on its own,

but so will experience, peer interaction, curiosity, and trial-and-error. Kids don't need to be constantly shaped to survive they need to be trusted

enough to shape themselves too.

THE ANSWER

Yes, adolescents need opportunities to make decisions, but the kind of autonomy research praises isn't raw freedom

it's guided autonomy. You can't trust a teen to navigate the world they haven't experienced yet.

My chapter doesn't advocate for blind obedience or micromanagement, it's about preparing them to make those independent choices responsibly.

Structure and guidance don't cancel out autonomy, they enable it safely. The truth is that teens will push boundaries no matter what.

Even in homes with warmth and balance, they test limits. A structured, faith-based environment isn't about punishment

it's about teaching responsibility in a safe space. The resentment often comes from inconsistency, not from firm boundaries paired with love.

My philosophy is precisely the balance of care and expectation, which research calls "authoritative parenting."

It's true that over-control can hurt self-esteem, but so can under-preparing a teen for reality.

My point is that teens' brains are reward-sensitive and inexperienced; letting them make every mistake freely risks real harm.

Shaping their character in a stable home teaches them to wield autonomy wisely, rather than leaving them to crash into harsh life lessons unprotected.

Structure without purpose or consistency is dangerous.

When structure is intentional, paired with moral and spiritual guidance, it equips teens to thrive, not just survive

Chapter 4

Kids love outside options….until they need you first

The notification hits my phone first.

$189.47 overdraft fee.

I freeze.

For a second, I think it's a glitch. I blink, refresh the banking app, squint like that's going to change the numbers. It doesn't.

The red minus sign is still there. Big. Loud. Disrespectful. My stomach drops. This isn't just a random charge. This is my *bill money* account.

The one I use for real life: lights, water, WiFi, all the quiet things that keep a house breathing. And someone just punched a hole in it.

I already know who.

A mother gets a sixth sense for this type of thing. "Algo huele raro aquí (something smells off here)," as abuela would say.

My generational instinct scram "yell"!!, "dale un fuetazo"!! Metle pa que aprenda!!

In other words beat their ass!! That's how they raised me…

I don't yell. Not yet. I walk out of my room and find him sprawled on the couch, headphones around his neck, laughing at something on his phone.

He's got that relaxed posture that only exists when you've never had a late fee in your life. I stand there for a moment, just watching.

He doesn't feel the storm yet. But the sky is already turning.

"Hey," I say, "Come here for a second." He looks up, half-annoyed, half-curious, the universal teenage expression.

"Yes ma, what happened?" he asks. I don't answer. Instead, I turn my phone toward him and let the number speak. His smile dies in real time.

You can literally see the shift; jaw tightens, shoulders lock, eyes widen. He reads it twice. "Is that… is that my fault?" he whispers.

There it is. That crack in the armor. "Why don't you tell me," I reply, still steady. "What did you buy?" He stares at the floor.

His thumb rubs the seam of his sweatpants, nervous. "A hoodie. Some shoes. A couple things," he mumbles. "A couple things where?" I ask.

"You used what?"

He swallows.

"Afterpay. Klarna. Whatever.   They said you could split it in four payments.   The YouTuber said it's smart 'cause it builds credit and stuff.

He said it's like free money if you keep up with it".   I close my eyes for half a second. *Ahí está (there it is)*. The "outside opinion."

Some influencer with ring lights and zero responsibility told him what to do with *my* account. I can feel the anger rise, hot, sharp, justified.

But layered underneath that is something heavier: Fear. Because this isn't about a hoodie. This is about a mindset.

He continues, words tumbling out now.

"They said parents don't understand how money works now, that y'all are stuck in old-school thinking. He said real hustlers use credit, not cash.

And besides". He stops.

"And besides what?" I press, eyebrows lifted.

"And besides… you always figure it out," he mutters.

There it is. The famous. "You always figure it out." In other words: *"I knew if it went wrong, you'd clean it up."* My heart pinches.

Not because he said it. Because part of him is right. I *do* always find a way.

I have pulled miracles out of thin air to keep these kids fed, housed, clothed, entertained. I've worked on four hours of sleep, made $20 stretch like a

full paycheck, smiled when I wanted to scream. They don't know that math. They just see the lights stay on and assume the universe runs on vibes.

"Escucha bien, nene" (listen carefully, son)," I say, voice dropping low. "La calle no te conoce, pero el banco sí.

(The streets don't know you, but the bank does.) And the bank? The bank doesn't play."

I tap the screen.

"See this number? This is not free money. This is a penalty. This is them charging me because *you* believed somebody who doesn't pay our bills."

He doesn't talk back.

"You know what hurts me?" I continue, softer but still firm. "It's not that you made a mistake. Everybody makes mistakes with money.

It's that you trusted a stranger to explain it instead of asking me first. You gave the internet more authority over our life than your own mother."

His eyes glass over.

"I didn't think it was that serious," he says. "No," I correct. "You didn't think *at all*." I sit on the arm of the couch.

I let the silence stretch. Not the passive-aggressive kind. the heavy, sacred kind that makes the truth echo.

"Let me ask you something," I continue. "If that YouTuber is wrong, does it cost him anything?" He shakes his head.

"If your little friend tells you, 'It's not that deep, just do it,' and it blows up, do they lose WiFi? Does their name go on the bill?

Do they stand in front of the light company explaining why the payment is late?" "No," he whispers.

"Exactly," I say. "Pero yo sí (but I do). I'm the one who has to fix this. I'm the one whose name is on the line."

I lean in, look him dead in the eyes.

"You can experiment with your image. You can experiment with your style. But you don't get to experiment with my survival." That lands.

You can feel it. He crumples a little, then finally asks the question that tells me his heart is still reachable: "What do we do now?"

"Now," I say, "we fix it together." His head snaps up. He wasn't expecting that.

"You're going to call the bank with me. You're going to listen to how overdraft fees work. You're going to watch me move the money, money

I was planning for something else…to cover this. And then, you're going to pay it back. Not because I need it…" I pause.

"…because *you* need to feel what it costs." He nods, slowly. "This isn't about punishing you," I add. "It's about teaching you. Porque como dicen,

'el que no aprende con palabras, aprende con golpe de realidad'. (because like they say, those who don't learn through words,

learn through blows of reality). I'd rather you feel the pain of a fee now than the pain of a foreclosure later."

His eyes widen again. "That's dramatic," he says weakly. "Life is dramatic," I reply. "I'm just the narrator."

Later that night, after the calls, after the rearranged payments, after the long breakdown of how overdrafts, credit, and "buy now, pay later"

really work, I lie in bed and stare at the ceiling. It would've been easier to just yell. It would've been quicker to just pay it and move on.

But I am not raising consumers. I am raising stewards. I am not raising babies.

I am raising future leaders who will one day be responsible for more than a hoodie.

Kids adore outside opinions. Right up until the moment those opinions cost them something real.

And when the bill arrives, when the consequences hit, when the anxiety starts, they don't run to the influencer.

They don't call the friend who hyped them up. They come to you. The parent. The anchor.

The one who has been telling them the truth all along. They don't always admit it. They don't always apologize right away.

But in those quiet, emotional moments when everything feels too heavy for them, their soul knows:

Mami no estaba mintiendo.

(Mom wasn't lying.)

"Plans fail for lack of counsel,
but with many advisers they succeed."
PROVERBS *15:22*

PRAYER FOR THIS CHAPTER

Dear God,

Thank You for giving me the privilege of guiding my children.

Grant me patience when they make mistakes, wisdom to teach without anger,

and strength to hold them accountable with love.

Help me show them the difference between fleeting advice and lasting truth.

Protect their hearts from blind trust in the world and teach them to seek Your counsel first.

Let me be steady when they stumble, firm when they test limits, and gentle when they fail.

May they learn responsibility, humility, and the value of consequences,

so they grow into wise, compassionate leaders.

Amen.

PRAYER FOR TEENS

God,

Help me make smart choices, even when others say differently.

Teach me to listen to the people who care about me, not just the ones online.

Give me the courage to admit mistakes and the wisdom to learn from them.

Help me understand that my actions have real consequences,

and let me see guidance as a gift, not a restriction.

Protect me from pride, impulsiveness, and shortcuts that seem easy but cost me later.

Thank You for my family and the love that guides me when life gets confusing.

Amen.

NEUROSCIENCE INSIGHT

WHY "EVERYBODY'S DOING IT" FEELS SAFER TO THEM THAN YOUR WARNING

The teenage brain is wired to chase **short-term reward** over long-term stability.

"Buy now, worry later" hits their dopamine system like sugar.

External voices (friends, influencers, older teens) feel "neutral,"

so the brain marks them as less emotionally threatening than a parent who carries history, emotion, and authority.

They underestim-ate risk because the **prefrontal cortex** (the part that handles planning and consequences)

is still developing well into their mid-twenties.

When a mistake impacts **real survival resources** (bills, rent, food, transportation), the brain encodes that experience more deeply

this is why letting them *feel* a safe version of consequence can permanently reshape their future decisions.

In simple terms:

Their brain is attracted to "fun, fast, and easy."

Your job is to anchor them in "real, steady, and safe" even when they don't like how it feels.

SIDEBAR FOR TEENS:

Think about it: when someone online tells you what to do, they **don't face the consequences**.

They won't feel the embarrassment if a decision backfires.
They won't lose privileges, miss deadlines, or deal with the fallout in real life.
They're giving advice with no real "skin in the game."

Your parents, teachers, and mentors? They **do** face the consequences not because they want control,

but because your actions affect the family, the home, and your future.

The lesson: not all advice is equal. Learn to weigh opinions based on who actually has to deal with the results.

Guidance from people who care isn't a restriction it's protection while you learn.

Ask yourself:

Does this person giving me advice lose anything if I mess up following it?

Are they just talking, or do they live what they preach?

Would they still tell me to do this if their name was on the account?

You don't have to obey blindly.

But if you're going to act grown, think like someone who has something to lose.

REFLECTION QUESTIONS

For Parents:

Have you ever fixed a financial mess your child created without letting them feel any of the impact? What did that teach them?

What outside voices influence your child the most when it comes to money and lifestyle?

How can you involve your teen in the real numbers, bills, fees, budgets, without shaming them?

What's one small, safe consequence you can let them experience so they begin to understand real-world cause and effect?

For Teens:

Have you ever spent money assuming "it'll work out" because someone else made it sound easy? What happened?

Do you treat your parent's income like a cushion or like something that has limits?

The last time your parent warned you about something money-related, how did you respond and what do you think about it now?

What's one financial decision you can ask your parent about *before* you make it?

THE REBUTTAL

"I get that you want teens to learn responsibility, but this reads like fear-based parenting.   You're essentially saying:
'If you don't listen to me, life will destroy you.'
That's a lot of pressure.

Not every decision a teen makes carries life-or-death consequences, and not every influencer's advice is harmful.   Part of growing up is experimenting, making mistakes, and learning from them, sometimes outside the safety net of a parent.

Also, framing mistakes as a 'lesson' that only works if they feel pain might make teens anxious or secretive.

Kids also learn responsibility through trust, modeling, and guided autonomy, not just watching consequences hit.
By insisting that they have to feel a direct consequence to internalize a lesson, you risk removing opportunities for judgment, self-reflection,
and independent decision-making.   They might follow rules out of fear of impact rather than understanding or wisdom.

Finally, your neuroscience explanation oversimplifies teen behavior. Teens often evaluate risk differently, but that doesn't mean they can't understand guidance or develop judgment before suffering a real penalty.

You might be underestimating their ability to think critically and overestimating the need for dramatic consequences."

THE ANSWER

I call it early intervention. And THAT'S why it's my job to teach them the truth before the world teaches it with fangs. I don't want a quiet child.

I want a wise one. Accountability saves more futures than comfort ever will. I'm raising adults who know how to manage money,

credit, impulse, risk, advice, and responsibility.

yes, teens are capable of critical thinking but their prefrontal cortex is still developing. Their brains crave reward and novelty, so risk often feels

abstract until they see the real, tangible consequences.

This method isn't about fear, it's about giving them a safe version of the hard truth so that when they face the real world,

they don't have to learn the same lesson under crisis.

In short: we're not replacing autonomy with control.

We're pairing guidance with responsibility in a way that sticks, teaching them how to weigh advice based on who actually has something to lose,

and how to make decisions that protect themselves and others.

Chapter 5

HOW TO BE THE PARENT THEY DENY BUT DEPEND

The door shuts harder than it needs to. Not slammed..just sharp enough to say: "I'm mad.   I don't want to hear you.   But also… don't go too far."

Teenagers are dramatic like that. Half warrior, half wounded bird, all attitude.   I stay in the hallway for a second, listening to the angry shuffle of feet

in their room.   The drawers open.   Something gets tossed. A deep breath.   Another.   Then silence

This isn't the silence of peace.

No.

This is the silence of processing, of pride fighting with vulnerability, of a teenager realizing they're mad at the one person. who would walk through fire for them. I lean my head against the wall and sigh. "Como decía mi abuela," I whisper to myself, "el hijo que más pelea contigo

es el que más necesita tu amor." ("The child who fights with you the most is the one who needs your love the most."). And it's true.

When they distance themselves emotionally, that's when they're most dependent on you not financially, but spiritually, mentally, psychologically.

Teenagers are wild. They'll deny you in public and depend on you in the dark. That's the paradox of raising them.

There's a knock inside their room soft, irregular, almost like a heartbeat on the wall. Then…. "Mami… can you come here?"

Just like that. All that anger? Gone. All that attitude? Evaporated. All that independence they swore they had? Where'd it go?

Deep down, beneath every eye roll and every "you don't get it" and every "leave me alone"…they're still your child. They still want your guidance.

Your reassurance. Your strength. Your presence. I open the door slowly, like a telenovela protagonist walking into a scene

that the audience already knows is about to break your heart.

They're sitting on the floor, knees pulled to their chest, pretending to look at something on their phone but dropping it the second they see me.

"Mami… I didn't mean what I said." And there it is. The crack in the façade. The truth. The dependence they swear they don't have.

I kneel beside them and say nothing. Sometimes silence is more powerful than any sermon. "Can you… just sit with me?" they ask.

And that's the moment a mother becomes not the villain, not the enemy, not the authority figure they want to rebel against but the anchor, the refuge,

the safe place, the living reminder that unconditional love still exists.

Teenagers deny us because they want to feel grown. They depend on us because deep down, they know they're not ready. This is why God made the bond between parent and child a spiritual contract, not a biological accident.

The truth is this:

You are the parent they reject out loud but rely on in silence.

They'll deny your advice… until the consequence hits.

They'll deny your warnings… until fear punches them in the gut.

They'll deny your rules… until life proves why you made them.

They'll deny your wisdom… until their heart breaks

Being that parent, the one they deny but depend on requires a different kind of strength. Not loud strength. Not "I'm the boss" strength.

Not "you need me" strength. But quiet, divine, steady strength. The kind backed by God, rooted in purpose,

held together by a spine forged in hardship. Because when they push us away the most is when they're secretly holding on the tightest.

I put my arm around my child. They relax instantly, resting their head against my shoulder like when they were small enough for me to carry.

"Mami," they whisper, "how do you stay so calm?"

I kiss the top of their head and smile. "Porque yo también necesitaba una mamá así," I say. ("Because I also needed a mother like this.")

They blink, surprised. And that's the truth behind all of this: You've become the parent you once prayed for. You've built the stability you never had.

You've given your children the softness you were denied, the patience nobody modeled for you, the guidance you had to learn the hard way.

They don't see that yet. But one day…they will. Until then…you stand firm. You love loud. You stay consistent.

You exist as the place they run back to when the world gets too loud for them to handle.

Because no matter how much they deny you, they depend on you with every breath they take in this house.

"Even if your father and mother abandon you, the Lord will hold you close."
PSALM *27:10*

A reminder that God is the strength behind every mother who stands alone.

PRAYER

"Lord,

 Help me be steady when my child is stormy. Grace me with patience when they push away, and clarity when their words are sharp.

 Teach me how to love them without fear, guide them without force, and protect them without controlling them. When they deny me,

 let me remember they still depend on me. When they push me away, let me remember they are reaching in their own way.

Cover our bond with Your peace and remind both of us that love never loses its place.

Amen."

PRAYER FOR TEENS

"God,

I'm frustrated and I don't always understand what's happening. Help me calm down and see things clearly.

Help me listen to my mom even when I don't want to. Give me patience and courage to ask for help when I need it.

Teach me to trust her guidance, and to remember she cares about me even when I'm mad or upset. Help me not push people away when

I need them the most.

Amen.

NEUROSCIENCE INSIGHT:

WHY TEENS ACT LIKE THEY DON'T NEED YOU EVEN WHEN THEY DO

The adolescent brain experiences **identity formation**, which makes them feel the need to "separate" from parents to become their own person.

But simultaneously, their limbic system (emotional brain) is overactive, so they depend on a parent's emotional regulation even while denying it.

Parent-child bond triggers oxytocin, the hormone of safety, which is why they come back to you during fear, sadness, or crisis.

Teens experience "ego expansion," making them *act mature* but feel fragile.

They push you away not because they don't need you

but because needing you feels like weakness to their developing identity.

Translation: They reject your help to prove independence, but they rely on your stability to survive emotional storms.

SIDEBAR FOR TEENS/TWEENS

Listen, corazón. That parent you argue with? That's the same parent you run to when something scares you.

You're not wrong for wanting independence. You're growing. It's normal. But don't confuse independence with isolation.

You can become your own person and still need guidance.

And needing your parent doesn't make you weak it makes you wise. Ask yourself: "If I didn't have this parent…

who would I be running to right now?" The answer tells you everything.

REFLECTION QUESTIONS

For Parents:

When was the last time your child pushed you away but later came to you for comfort?

How do you usually react when they deny needing you?

What kind of emotional anchor do you want to be for your child?

How can you create space for your teen to feel safe returning to you?

For Teens:

Why is it easier to push your parent away than to admit you need them?

When was the last time you depended on your parent without saying it?

What scares you about needing guidance?

In what areas of your life could you accept help without feeling "childish"?

Chapter 6

WHEN GENTLE PARENTING ISN'T ENOUGH

The house is loud tonight. Not with noise…with energy. That thick tension you can feel in the walls, like the air itself is holding its breath

because someone's fuse is half an inch long. I'm standing at the stove warming dinner, and behind me I feel the first storm rise. My youngest stomps

down the hallway, jaw clenched, eyes blazing like a match looking for a reason to ignite. "I want to be left alone!!" Her voice slices through the air

sharp, emotional, trembling the kind of tone that tells you she's trying to hold herself together and losing.

"¿Qué pasó, mi amor?" (What happened, my love?). She won't look at me.

Hands curled in tight fists. Breathing fast like her anger has its own heartbeat. "Mami, I don't know what's wrong with me!

I get MAD for no reason… like something explodes inside me!" And right there, I see myself at her age, I see her father as well…fighting a fire

nobody taught me to name. She doesn't know that part of her rage is inherited. A family trait passed down like eye color or cheekbones or musicality.

She doesn't understand that she's wrestling with ghosts that once lived inside me, inside her dad. I kneel in front of her, not touching her

not yet. Kids like her, kids wired to feel intensely, need space before contact. I speak low. I say. "You're overwhelmed." She looks up, startled,

as if those words slipped a key into a locked door. "Your anger didn't start with you, but YOU get to end it."

She takes a shuddered breath and the storm softens. Not gone. Just softer. I don't rescue her from the feeling. I sit beside it with her.

Because some children listen to calm words. Others? They listen to calm presence. And tonight, she needs both. She's mourning the loss of her father.

Meanwhile Another Storm Breaks. The middle child walks in dragging a blanket like it's evidence of a crime.

"Mami, she messed up my room again!" I don't even respond, my brain is still processing my youngest's meltdown but Im certain

God must've assigned me the Advanced Edition of motherhood. I turn to him, eyeing the blanket. "Why is it on the floor?" I ask. He blinks.

He wasn't ready for that plot twist.

Earlier, he had spent a solid hour building a fortress out of pillows and blankets in the middle of his room. It wasn't just a mess it was *his space*,
carefully arranged, a little world where he could play, read, or just be himself without interruptions.

Then his older sibling came through. They didn't mean anything by it, just stepped over the edge of the fort, and in one careless motion, sent half of
it tumbling to the floor. Books scattered. Pillows fell. His carefully folded blanket landed in a heap. To anyone else, it's a minor accident. To him,
it's an invasion, a personal violation, a betrayal of the time and care he put into creating something just for him. That's why he's dragging the
blanket now, muttering under his breath, because to him it's *evidence* proof that someone doesn't respect what he values.

Alright," I say finally, my voice low and steady. "Show me what happened." I follow him into the room, eyes scanning the wreckage. Pillows askew. Books scattered. The blankets crumpled in the corner.

"Okay," I say, crossing my arms. "I see it. I get why you're upset. You worked hard to make this space yours. And yeah, someone messed it up."
"She…she didn't even say sorry!"

"No," I say. "She didn't. And I know that stings. That's life. Sometimes people don't care about what you care about,
or they just don't notice. That doesn't make it okay, but it does mean you get to choose how to handle it."

I pull a pillow off the floor, and toss it back onto the fort. "You can yell. You can stomp. You can pout. But dragging the blanket around the house
like it's a crime scene? That's just giving the problem more power than it deserves. You fix your space, take a breath, and then you decide
if you want to talk to her…or not. But you don't let this ruin your day."

He stares at me, chest heaving, fists slowly unclenching. For the first time since he came in, he looks like he's considering the idea that he *does* have control over how this ends. I don't pat his head. I don't say "it's okay." I let him own the feeling. I let him know the storm is real but he doesn't have to drown in it.

Then comes the oldest, betrayal bleeding through her eyes. She walks in quietly, holding her phone like it's a broken heart that's still warm.

Her voice cracks. "Mami… she blocked me." And that's all it takes. I know exactly which friend. The one she worries about. The one she warned.

The one she tried to protect with honesty that wasn't asked for but was needed.

"What happened?" I ask. She sinks onto the couch. Her shoulders collapse. Looking at the floor…. "I told her he sounded wrong.

That the way he texted was manipulative. And she got mad. She said I was jealous. She said I wanted him. And then" ….She swallows hard.

"she blocked me everywhere." Ay, mi reina… Teenage betrayal is its own funeral. No casket. No flowers. Just silence and screenshots and a heaviness

adults forget. I sit beside her. "You weren't jealous," I say. "I know," she whispers. "You saw danger she couldn't see." Tears glide down her cheeks.

"I was trying to save her…" I cup her face gently. "People don't listen when their fantasy feels better than your truth. "She nods, and that single

movement breaks my heart. Because this is the lesson I cannot protect her from. Some warnings cost friendships. Some truths cost comfort.

Some betrayals give wisdom. I braid a loose strand of her hair behind her ear and kiss her forehead. "One day she'll understand," I whisper.

"But today you let the pain teach what the words couldn't." She'll come around, you just wait. You are a great friend, she's just blinded by "love"

love does that sometime. I yell out loud!! "My beautiful children, who would like some chocolate Cortez with quest de papa!!??

They all come running forgetting all the troubles they felt… "I do, I do"

And Then… My own lesson finds me. When the house finally quiets, when all three storms return to their bedrooms, I sit at the kitchen table with

my hands over my face. Because raising kids alone is not one job it's a thousand invisible jobs stacked on top of each other. It takes a village

And tonight… like most nights, I worked all of them at once. Three children. Three emotional earthquakes. Three different needs.

Three different wounds. And in the middle of all that? I realized how easy it is to abandon myself trying to rescue everyone else.

I learned something tonight:

I can soothe.

I can teach.

I can discipline.

I can guide.

I can love fiercely.

But I cannot save them from the lessons their souls signed up for. I am the mother, not the shield. And sometimes the most loving thing

I can do is stand beside the storm instead of blocking it. I exhale a long breath.

"Mami no estaba mintiendo," I whisper to myself. And neither were they. Their pain was real. Their anger was real. Their confusion was real.

And God trusted **me** to guide them through it without losing myself. I close my eyes and feel the peace seep in. Tonight taught all four of us.

And that is the beauty of the lessons we can't rescue them from.

**"The Lord is close to the brokenhearted
 and saves those who are crushed in spirit."**
PSALM *34:18*

PRAYER

"Father,

Give me wisdom for the storms I cannot stop and patience for the children who carry battles they didn't create. Teach me to guide without rescuing,

to love without absorbing, to discipline without wounding, and to rest without guilt. Cover my children's hearts as they learn to calm their storms,

own their choices, and trust their intuition. And remind me, Lord, that even when I am tired, you are the strength that holds this home.

Amen."

NEUROSCIENCE INSIGHT:

WHEN CALM WORDS CAN'T BE HEARD

Kids from chaotic or inconsistent environments develop a brain pattern called:

"Emotional Noise Interference."

This means:

They can't process calm words when their nervous system is in survival mode.

The amygdala (fear/anger center) hijacks logic.

The prefrontal cortex (reasoning) shuts down temporarily.

They react before they understand.

They defend before they hear.

They explode before they think. Gentle parenting does not work when the child's brain is stuck in survival mode.

Instead:

✓ Firm structure

✓ Predictability

✓ Emotional regulation

✓ Consistent boundaries

✓ Presence without panic

✓ Consequences without cruelty

…these rewire the nervous system from chaos to calm.

You don't fix them. You MODEL safety until their brain learns safety.

SIDEBAR FOR TEENS/ KIDS

Your anger, sadness doesn't make you a bad person.

It means your feelings are bigger than your words.

Your mistakes don't define you. Your growth does.

Your mom isn't trying to control you. She's trying to protect you

from losing pieces of yourself to people who don't deserve them.

Before you push her away, ask:

"Is she the only person who would fight for me in this situation?"

If the answer is yes, you're not alone.   You're blessed.

REFLECTION QUESTIONS

For Parents:

Where have you been over-rescuing your children to avoid discomfort?

Which of your child's patterns trigger old wounds in YOU?

How can you guide without absorbing their emotional weight?

What personal lesson did YOU learn while helping them learn theirs?

For Teens:

What feeling hits you fastest? anger, fear, or embarrassment? Why?

When someone warns you about a situation, do you listen or defend?

What lesson are you currently avoiding because it feels hard?

How can you help yourself calm down before reacting next time?

THE REBUTTAL

"Okay but… seriously? Why make such a big deal about teenagers having emotions? Kids get mad. Kids get overwhelmed. Kids cry, scream,

slam doors, and say things they don't mean. It's part of growing up. Why are you treating every little argument like it's a trauma cycle or

some spiritual inheritance?

Why bring up 'inherited anger'? Why talk about ghosts and emotional wiring? You're giving too much meaning to normal teenage attitude.

Kids get mad for no reason. It doesn't have to be deeper than that. Then the middle one? Why turn a simple blanket on the floor into a whole

accountability lesson?

Why can't he forget something without it becoming some philosophical exploration? And your oldest, a friend blocking her? That's life.

Kids lose friends every day.   Why make everything a spiritual sign?   Why make everything a generational wound?   Why act like these moments

are destiny-shaping?   And why end the chapter talking about YOUR lesson for the night?   Isn't this supposed to be about the kids?

Why weave faith, psychology, boundaries, trauma, and emotional literacy into what could've been a five-minute parenting moment?

Why can't you just say: 'Teenagers have moods.   They get over it.'   Why complicate it?   Isn't this too dramatic?

Aren't you reading too much into things?   Aren't you making parenting harder than it needs to be?"

THE ANSWER

I'm not dramatizing motherhood. I'm paying attention to what MOST parents ignore.

You think these moments are small because you never learned to see the roots beneath the reaction. You were raised in environments where kids

were punished, not understood.

Where emotions were mocked, not named. Where silence was survival, not calm.

Where anger was called disrespect instead of untreated generational trauma. And I refuse to repeat that cycle.

When my child shakes with anger, I don't see disrespect I see a nervous system overwhelmed by inheritance and environment.

When my son avoids responsibility, I don't see laziness I see learned patterns that will shape his adulthood if I don't address them.

When my daughter bleeds betrayal, I don't see drama, I see the beginning of her emotional boundaries forming right in front of me.

You say:

'It's normal. Kids get over it.'

And LOOK at our society… Kids "got over it" and grew into adults who:

– shut down instead of communicating

– explode instead of expressing

– self-sabotage instead of self-regulate

– choose toxic partners over stable ones

– mistake chaos for love

– react instead of reflect

– wound their own kids the way they were wounded

So no…

I won't minimize ANY of it. Because every 'small moment' is an entrance into a root. And every root will eventually grow fruit.

I'm not raising kids to just 'get over it.' I'm raising kids to understand it, heal it, navigate it, and transform it.

I don't kneel to coddle them. I kneel to CONNECT with them before correcting them. I don't 'complicate' parenting. I clarify it.

I don't overanalyze. I decode. I don't dramatize. I discern. And that's why God trusted ME with these three souls. You say it's too much.

I say it's necessary. Because I'm not raising kids to survive childhood… I'm raising adults who won't repeat mine."

Chapter 7

THE APOLOGIES COME LATER

You can tell when a child is about to apologize before they even open their mouth. Not because you're psychic

(but let's be honest, motherhood is its own kind of prophecy) but because their energy shifts. Their shoulders soften.   Their eyes keep dragging toward

you then away then back again.   Their breathing calms from thunder to rain to drizzle.   But the words? The words take longer.   Because apologies

are not born from pride.   They're born from reflection. And reflection only happens when the storm inside them finally gets tired.

The morning after the storm.   The house is unusually quiet. Not peaceful quiet more like when la protagonista in a telenovela wakes up after the

episode where she flipped a table, threw what's at hands reach, accused everyone of betrayal, and now she's mortified.

That kind of quiet.

One by one, my kids drift out of their rooms.

Youngest: eyes swollen from the anger meltdown she swore she didn't need help with.

Middle: walking carefully, as if respect can be stepped on or honored.

Oldest: moving softly, still wounded from the betrayal she felt… still embarrassed she didn't listen to her own intuition.

Nobody looks at me at first. Not directly… And that's how you know the apology is loading. Because when kids are ready to say sorry,

they don't walk up and announce it. They orbit you. They test the air. They calculate risk. They feel the energy in the room,

to see if you're still mad, still disappointed, or still hurt. But the thing they don't know is this:

A mother forgives her children before they even cause the damage. The Youngest Goes First.   She stands in the doorway, arms crossed,

brows knit trying to decide between pride and peace. "Mami…" she whispers. Just that one word.   But I know the rest.   She comes closer.

Then rests her head against my arm.   Her voice breaks. "I didn't mean to yell…" I wrap her in my arms like the child she still is beneath all that fire.

"I know," I say. "And you're learning.   Así se empieza." (That's how it starts.)   She exhales the first apology she didn't know how to form last night.

The middle child's turn,   He slides into the kitchen with the slow steps of a teen, pretending to be relaxed but clearly rehearsing something.

He grabs a bowl.   Pours cereal.   Pretends the spoon is fascinating. Then: "Mami, I cleaned my room."

"Did you do it because I asked," I say, "or because you realized it needed to be done?" He swallows. "The second one."   There it is. I nod.

"That's what responsibility feels like."   He looks at me, "Sorry for giving you attitude," he adds.   I don't scold him.   I don't lecture.

I don't stack guilt on top of guilt. (Just because I was brought up being yelled at and beat everyday that way doesn't always mean that's the right way.

There's more than one way to find a solution)

I simply respond: "I appreciate your honesty." Apologies bloom faster when shame isn't choking the soil.

The oldest comes last. She walks toward me slowly, like a woman carrying her own heartbreak carefully, so it doesn't spill. "Mami…" she murmurs.

She sits beside me the way someone sits beside a person they trust with their soul. "I should've listened to you," she says. "I warned her…

but I didn't protect myself. And I don't know why it hurts so much." I take her hand. "Because loyalty lives deeper in you than people expect."

She wipes a tear. "I'm sorry for snapping at you," she says. "I didn't mean to take it out on you." I kiss her forehead.

"If your sadness comes to me first," I say, "that means I'm still your safe place." She gives me a big hug and walks back to her room.

Just before entering I tell her… "Yeah, but don't get used to (taking it out on me) you're getting older. It's time you start learning self control ok mamita?"

What they don't know: A mother's apology comes first. Before they apologized to me, I had already apologized to myself for believing

I had to be perfect for them to learn. Motherhood taught me this: Children apologize late because understanding comes late.

But late doesn't mean empty. Late doesn't mean fake. Late doesn't mean ungrateful. It means human. And the reason their apologies feel

powerful is because they come from a place they finally had to visit: reflection.

They come later because the lesson comes first.

"A gentle answer turns away wrath,
 but a harsh word stirs up anger."
  PROVERBS *15:1*

PRAYER

"Father,

Teach my children humility without shame, growth without guilt, and reflection without fear. Help me guide them with patience

as they learn to repair what they break with maturity and grace. Let our home be a place where apologies heal instead of reopen wounds.

And remind me that love is strongest when forgiveness is offered before the words are spoken.

Amen."

PRAYER FOR TEENS

God,
I messed up. I see it, even if I don't feel like saying it out loud yet.
Help me fix what I can, own what I can, and learn from the rest.
Give me the guts to face the consequences without whining.
Teach me to think before I speak, act, or snap.
Remind me that growing up isn't about being perfect, it's about being honest, even when it's hard.
Let me get stronger, wiser, and kinder before the

apology comes.
Amen.

NEUROSCIENCE INSIGHT: WHY APOLOGIES COME LATE

Your brain has a few main "zones," and when you're upset or mad, some of them literally shut down:

Amygdala: This is your emotional alarm system. When it goes off, it hijacks your brain so you feel the storm before you think.

Prefrontal cortex: This is your "decision-making boss." When emotions are raging, it takes a back seat. That's why you say stuff you regret.

Insula: Your self-awareness center. It checks in with your feelings and body, but when you're heated, it's basically asleep.

Anterior cingulate cortex (ACC): The "error alert system." It doesn't fully wake up until the storm is over. Once it's online, you finally see what went wrong, why you acted that way, and how to fix it.

Translation: When you're mad, sad, or stressed, your brain isn't broken, it's just in survival mode.

Reflection, apologies, and learning happen *after* the storm, not during it. That's why it's smart to step back, breathe, and wait before reacting.

This means:

✓ Kids cannot apologize while dysregulated

✓ They must decompress first

✓ Once calm, the brain rewires through reflection

✓ Apologies become more genuine *after* emotional recovery

Apologies come late because understanding comes late. It's biology, not rebellion.

SIDEBAR FOR TEENS/KIDS

You don't have to be perfect to say "I'm sorry." Your parents aren't waiting for perfect. They're waiting for honesty.

Saying sorry doesn't make you weak. It makes you trustworthy. It makes you wise. It makes you human.

Next time you mess up, ask:

"What did I learn from this that I didn't understand before?" That's where the real apology begins.

REFLECTION QUESTIONS

For Parents:

How do you feel when apologies come late?

Do you allow your child space to reflect before expecting an apology?

How can you model healthy repair during conflict?

What is one apology you've been carrying that you need to release?

For Teens:

Why is apologizing hard for you?

How does your body feel when you know you need to say sorry?

What lesson did your last conflict teach you?

How can you repair trust without feeling embarrassed?

THE REBUTTAL
The One Who "Doesn't Get Why This Matters

"Okay but…isn't all this a bit TOO emotional? Kids apologize. Parents forgive. Conflict happens. That's life. Why turn a simple 'I'm sorry'

into this whole dramatic process? Why talk about nervous systems, emotions, spiritual bonds and psychological timing?

Why analyze the silence, the breathing, the body language? Why act like an apology is some sacred ritual? Back in the day, kids apologized

immediately or they got consequences. Nobody waited for 'reflection.' Nobody talked about 'regulation.' Nobody knelt down and

watched their child breathe. Parents didn't do all this emotional interpretation. Kids said sorry because they had to. And it worked. So why do you

make everything so deep? Maybe they're not reflecting, maybe they're just embarrassed. Maybe they're not growing or they just don't like being in trouble. Maybe you're over-philosophizing simple teenage behavior. Why not just accept the apology and keep it moving?

Why turn the morning after into a spiritual revelation? Isn't all this too dramatic…too intense…too symbolic?

Why can't apologies just be… apologies?"

THE ANSWER

I'm not making apologies dramatic. I'm honoring WHAT THEY REALLY ARE. You think an apology is just words.

I think an apology is growth in motion. You think it's just a moment. I know it's a milestone. You think I'm overthinking.

I think you're under-feeling.

Listen carefully:

Kids don't apologize late because they're stubborn. They apologize late because their nervous system literally cannot access humility until after the storm passes.   You think immediate apologies equal respect.   But immediate apologies often equal FEAR.   I don't want fearful children.

I want reflective ones.   I don't want kids who say sorry to escape consequences.   I want kids who say sorry because they understand impact.

You say:

'Parents didn't do all that psychological stuff before.' Yes, and look at the emotional damage their generation carried into adulthood.

Silence masquerading as obedience.   Fear masquerading as respect.   Trauma masquerading as discipline.   Suppression masquerading as strength.

I'm not repeating that.

You say I'm making apologies sacred.   I say yes because they ARE.

An apology is not:
 – compliance
 – embarrassment

– submission

– convenience

An apology is:

– reflection

– humility

– emotional intelligence

– accountability

– nervous system maturity

– relational repair

And THAT is what I'm teaching my children. Not how to perform obedience…but how to practice growth. Connection comes before correction

and correction without connection breeds rebellion. You think I analyze too much.   I think you avoid feeling.   You think I dramatize.

I think you minimize. You ask why apologies matter so deeply?   Because apologies are not the end of conflict they are the beginning of understanding.

And THAT is how generational change begins."

Chapter 8

THE ART OF SAYING NOTHING AND STILL WINNING

Hay días en que una madre no tiene que abrir la boca pa' ganar. Solo respira.   Se cruza de brazos. Levanta una ceja.   Y boom

KO instantáneo.

No words needed. No speeches. No novela monólogo. Just… that mothers glare, that look…. Esa misma. La que paraliza células.

La que detiene terremotos.   La que hace que los nenes regresen sin tú llamarlos. La que dice: "Pórtate bien… o te alineo sin usar las manos."

En Puerto Rico no se educa con gritos solamente. A veces se educa con telepatía ancestral.

Mira pa' allá el nene iba a responder, pero con un *"mami, te juro que no fui yo"* atorado en la boca, se quedó frizao'

porque vio tu ceja subiendo como ascensor sin frenos.

Esa es la magia. *La ciencia moderna no está lista pa' esto.* Hoy, los tres míos están en modo:

"Déjala quieta que está con la mirada heavy." Tú sabes cuál:

La chiquita entra a la sala con esa energía algaretosa. *Mala combinación con hambre, sueño, y ser hija mía.* "Mami, ¿puedo…..?" Yo no digo nada.

Solo miro. Ella se detiene en seco. Se endereza. Traga hondo. "Está bien… ya sé," y se va directa a hacer lo que tenía que hacer desde

hace tres horas. Sin pelea. Sin drama. Sin "¿por qué yo?" Nada.

La Mirada Elimina la actitud. *Super efectiva. Pokémon level.*

El Niño y la Mirada del Respeto. Él quiere contestar. Tiene una opinión. La veo formándose. El pecho se le infla. La boca se le abre

Yo giro el cuello lentamente, tipo *villana de novela mexicana,* y lo miro por encima del lente del alma.

Cerró la boca.   Cerró la actitud.   Cerró el capítulo. "Voy a recoger mi cuarto, Mami."   Sin tú decir una sola sílaba.

Ese es el poder que no se enseña.   Ese se hereda.   Ese viene del linaje de mujeres que criaron hijos con chancleta muteada y disciplina wireless.

La grande llega con cara de novela triste. Como si Ana Isabelle estuviera cantando de fondo.   Se sienta al lado mío.   No habla.

Solo respira profundo.   Las emociones bailando salsa en su pecho.   Yo no pregunto nada.   Solo pongo mi mano encima de la suya y la miro.

Mi mirada dice: "Cuéntame cuando estés lista."

"No te voy a juzgar."

"No eres loca."

"No eres mala amiga."

"No eras tú."

"Estoy aquí."

Habla. Se desahoga. Y cuando termina, se acuesta en mi hombro como cuando era chiquita y pensaba que yo lo podía arreglar todo. Yo no dije nada.

Pero gané su confianza sin luchar por ella.

Ese es el arte.

Ese es el poder.

Ese es el secreto.

A veces necesitas palabras.

A veces necesitas sabiduría.

Pero hay momentos en que la victoria viene del silencio, del control, del aura, del espíritu que camina contigo.

Porque una madre que domina el silencio domina la casa entera.

(I had to throw in Spanish for the one) wink wink

Here's the English version:

Some days, a mother doesn't need to open her mouth to win. She just breathes.   Crosses her arms.   Raises an eyebrow.
And boom instant knockout…KO

No words. No lectures. No telenovela monologues. Just… that motherly glare, *that look*.   The one that freezes cells, stops earthquakes,
and makes kids come running back without being called.

The one that says: "Behave… or I'll straighten you out without touching you."

In Puerto Rico, raising kids isn't always about yelling. Sometimes it's done with ancestral telepathy.

He opens her mouth to respond, "Mami, I swear it wasn't me…". and freezes mid-word, because he sees your eyebrow rising like an
elevator with no brakes. That's the magic.   Modern science isn't ready for this.

Today, all three of mine are in full: "Better leave her alone she's in *the look* mode."   You know which one.

The little one walks into the living room with that chaotic energy bad combo of hunger, sleep deprivation, and being my daughter.
"Mom, can I…?"

I don't say a word. Just look. She stops in her tracks. Straightens up. Swallows hard. "Okay… I got it," and goes straight to do what she was supposed to do three hours ago.
No fight. No drama. No "why me?" Nothing.

The Look Eliminates attitude. Super effective. Pokémon level.

The Kid and the Look of Respect.   He wants to answer back.   He has an opinion forming.   Chest puffed. Mouth opening. I turn my head slowly, like a villain in a Mexican telenovela, and look at him over the lens of the soul. Mouth shuts.   Attitude shuts.   Chapter closed.
"I'm going to clean my room, Mom."

Not a word from me. That's the power they don't teach you.

It's inherited. It comes from a lineage of women who raised children with muted flip-flops and wireless discipline.

The oldest walks in with the face of a sad telenovela star, like Ana Isabelle singing in the background.   She sits next to me.   Doesn't speak.
Just breathes, emotions dancing salsa in her chest.   I don't ask a thing.   Just put my hand on hers and look at her.

My eyes say:
"Tell me when you're ready."
"I won't judge you."
"You're not crazy."
"You're not a bad friend."
"It wasn't you."
"I'm here."

She speaks.   She empties herself.   And when she's done, she lies on my shoulder like she used to when she was little, believing I could fix everything.

I didn't say a word.   But I earned her trust without a fight.

That's the art.
That's the power.
That's the secret.

Sometimes words are necessary. Sometimes wisdom is needed. But there are moments when victory comes from silence, control, aura, and presence.

Because a mother who masters silence… masters the entire house.

"Be quick to listen, slow to speak, and slow to anger."
JAMES 1:19

PRAYER

"Señor,

Dame la sabiduría de saber cuándo hablar

y el discernimiento de saber cuándo quedarme callada.

Permite que mi silencio sea guía,

mi mirada sea frontera,

y mi presencia sea paz.

Enséñame a ganar batallas sin pelear,

a corregir sin herir,

y a amar sin forzar.

Amén."

God,

Give me the wisdom to know when to speak

and the discernment to know when to stay silent.

Let my silence be a guide,

my gaze a boundary,

and my presence a source of peace.

Teach me to win battles without fighting,

to correct without hurting,

and to love without forcing.

Amen."

NEUROSCIENCE INSIGHT: WHY SILENCE WORKS

The teen brain reacts VERY differently depending on your approach:

✓ Words during conflict = perceived threat. Their amygdala fires, hearing attack, not guidance.

✓ Silence + presence = emotional regulation. Your calm body becomes a co-regulator, lowering their stress hormones.

✓ Eye contact activates the prefrontal cortex. It literally forces logical thinking to turn back on.

✓ A calm parent resets the child's nervous system. Without saying a word, your presence rewires their response.

✓ Silence stops the "power struggle loop". Because the fight only happens if BOTH sides talk.

Translation:

You aren't being passive…

you're being strategic, neurologically superior, and spiritually gangster.

SIDEBAR FOR TEENS/KIDS

Sometimes your mom looking at you like that

is not her wanting to fight. It's her saying:

"I know you better than you know yourself." You think she's mad?

Half the time she's reading your energy like a detective mixed with Google mixed with the Holy Spirit.

The silence isn't punishment. It's space.

Space for YOU to think before you talk.

Space to calm down.

Space to make a better choice before the chancla becomes a prophecy.

REFLECTION QUESTIONS

For Parents:

When was the last time silence won a battle for you?

Do you react too fast verbally?

What situations in your home require LESS talking and MORE presence?

Which "look" of yours is most effective, and why?

For Teens:

What do you feel when your parent goes silent?

Does silence make you think more clearly or make you defensive?

What message do you think your parent is sending with their mirada?

How can you pause before reacting next time?

THE REBUTTAL

"Pero why make it so dramatic? It's just a look."
"Girl, relax. It's just a LOOK. Every mom gives their kid a stare sometimes.

Why turn it into this whole spiritual-co-regulation-neuroscience-Superpower? Kids need words. Kids need explanations.

Kids need full conversations. Not… silent novelas in the kitchen. Why act like silence is some ancient Boricua technique? It's just parenting.

If a kid stops their attitude because you looked at them, that's intimidation, not wisdom. Why not talk it out? Why not explain?

Why not communicate? Isn't that what you've been saying? This whole 'silence wins' things… Doesn't it teach kids to fear you?

Doesn't it make them read your mood instead of your words? And come on… the mirada? The look…Really?

You're romanticizing something simple. Silence doesn't raise kids. Communication does. A mother crossing her arms and lifting an eyebrow isn't psychology. It's attitude. So why make it poetic? Why not just SAY what you need to say instead of acting like you're a Jedi

with chancla powers?"

THE ANSWER

You think silence is empty because you've never understood power without noise. Let me explain something:

A LOOK is not intimidation.

A LOOK is regulation.

A LOOK is not fear.

A LOOK is boundary.

A LOOK is not controlling.

A LOOK is connecting the nervous system of a calm mother, to the nervous system of a dysregulated child without escalating the storm.

You say:

'Just explain.' But what you don't know is this:

A child cannot hear logic while drowning in emotion. Words are gasoline when the brain is on fire. Silence is water.

In my culture, and in many others, our mothers taught with presence long before they taught with speeches. Because presence grounds. Words overwhelm.

It's ancestral.

It's psychological.

It's spiritual.

It's biological.

It's cultural.

It's instinctual.

You see a look. I see a download:

The wisdom of every mother before me activated in my face before I even open my mouth.

You see intimidation. I see interruption of chaos.

You see attitude. I see alignment.

I see truth spoken without noise, the highest form of discipline and self-control.

You ask:

'Why not talk?' Because sometimes words make the child fight harder. Sometimes silence helps them reflect. Sometimes a pause

teaches more than a paragraph. Sometimes the mirada says:

I'm here.

I'm calm.

I see you.

I'm not matching your chaos.

But you WILL match my peace."

You fear silence. I mastered it. You think silence is lack of communication. I know silence is communication for those who know how to listen.

My silence is not threatening. It's guiding. Not punishment. Preparation. Not fear. Formation. Not intimidation. But intuition.

If you think the mirada is "just a look," that tells me one thing:

No one ever taught you the language of presence. But don't worry. By the time you finish this book, you'll be fluent.

Chapter 9

WHEN YOU STOP SAVING THEM, THEY START THINKING

The morning starts like a "Caso Cerrado" episode, quiet on the surface, but you can FEEL the drama warming up like arroz con gandules.

My youngest is pacing the kitchen, my middle child is slumped on the couch pretending to be invisible, and my oldest is staring at her phone

And me? I'm in my mother-warrior mode: calm face, tight bun, and a cup of my favorite tea.

Because today…nobody gets rescued.

"Buenos días," I say sweetly.   Three heads snap up like deer in headlights.   Most kids know: when Mami is this calm?

Corre. (Run.)

The Youngest: "Figure It Out" Begins

She storms in, hair wild, mood wilder. "Mami, can you help me find my shoes?! I can't find NOTHING!" I sip my tea Slow…Villainess slow.

"¿Y tus pies dónde están?" (And where are your feet?). She blinks. Then: "Mami, stop! I'm LATE!" I shrug. "Pues busca." (So look.)

She freezes. She expected the usual: me running around, digging under couches, moving furniture like a CrossFit champion. But not today. Today,

I let the panic teach her. Let the frustration guide her. Let the natural consequence warm up. She stomps away. Fires every drawer.

Throws a jacket. Yells at a sock. And right before she explodes.. She finds the shoes. She stops. Stares at them. Then at me.

"Mami… I found them." I smile softly. "Claro que sí," I say. "Porque you're more capable than your attitude."

Her eyes widen lesson learned, zero yelling required.

The Middle Child: The Chore Catastrophe

He walks in with "el moco colgando," looking like a rejected telenovela extra. "Mami… I forgot to take out the trash and now the bag broke."

I take a slow sip. "Oh. ¿Y qué vas a hacer?" (What are you going to do?). He blinks. "Yo? Pero". "No hay pero." (No "but.")

"You left it. You fix it."

"Mami, but it STINKS!" He whines

"Pues ponte guantes." (Then put on gloves.) He stands there, processing the betrayal. This is the moment his brain wakes up.

This is the moment he realizes: Mami isn't the janitor. Mami isn't the fixer. Mami isn't the last-minute rescue squad.

Mami is the guide.

He goes off muttering refranes he invents on the spot like: "Esto es abuso emocional…" (This is emotional abuse…)

But after seven minutes of whining, the trash is OUT. The floor is mopped. His face is cleaner than the kitchen.

And his attitude? Suddenly humbled.

The Lost Homework. My oldest comes in, panicked: "Mami… I can't find my homework folder. I think I left it at school!"

Normally, I'd jump. Retrace steps, call the office, text the teacher, maybe even drive back to school. Rescue mode: full blast.

But today? Not today.

I look at her and ask one question: "¿Qué vas a hacer tú?" (What are YOU going to do?). She blinks at me, wide-eyed. "Uh… I guess…
check my backpack again? Call my friend to see if they have it?"

I nod. "Good. Try that first." She spends the next ten minutes rifling through every pocket, texting her friends, retracing her mental steps.

Finally, she finds it crumpled under the couch cushions. Her face lights up. Relief, pride, and..best of all…she did it. She solved it.
I didn't save her. I didn't swoop in. I just let her figure it out.

And the win? She sat down for dinner that evening with a little extra spring in her step, knowing she could handle small disasters on her own.

Galatians 6:5

"For each one should carry his own load." We're called to own our actions instead of relying on others to fix everything.

PRAYER

"Lord,

Help me let go of the fear that makes me overprotect.

Teach me to trust the lessons You place in my children's path.

Give them courage to face challenges without collapsing,

and wisdom to recognize their own strength.

Let struggle shape them,

not break them.

Amén."

PRAYER FOR TEENS

Owning My Choices

God, help me see my choices clearly.
Give me courage to do what's right, even when it's hard.
Teach me to learn from my mistakes, not hide from them.
Help me respect those who care for me, even when I don't understand them.
Let me feel the consequences of my actions safely, so I grow stronger and wiser.
Give me patience with myself, humility in my victories, and grace in my failures.
Thank You for guiding me, even when I don't ask, and for loving me through every step of learning.
Amen.

NEUROSCIENCE INSIGHT:

WHY NOT SAVING THEM WORKS

Struggle activates the **prefrontal cortex**, building maturity.

Completing tasks alone boosts **dopamine**, increasing motivation.

Solving problems without help develops **executive function** (decision-making).

Not rescuing teaches the brain:

"I can handle discomfort."

Which destroys entitlement and builds resilience.

TEEN SIDEBAR/KIDS

When your mom doesn't jump in to save you,

she's not abandoning you. She's promoting you.

She's telling you: "Tú puedes." (You can.)

Because if she does everything for you,

you'll never know what you're capable of.

REFLECTION QUESTIONS

<u>For Parents:</u>

What situations do you rescue too quickly?

What fears make you overprotect?

Which child needs more space to learn?

How can you let struggle teach without abandoning?

<u>For Teens:</u>

What task do you avoid because it feels "too hard"?

How did you feel the last time you solved something alone?

Who are you when nobody rescues you?

What can you try doing solo this week?

THE REBUTTAL

"So you're just letting them struggle? That's harsh."
"Pero chica…. why would you let your child struggle like that?

Why let the youngest panic over shoes when you could've just helped? Why let the middle one gag over trash instead of doing it yourself?

Why let your oldest sit in silence when she's clearly hurt? Isn't that cold? Isn't that unloving? Isn't that…. too much?

Kids need help. Kids need support. Kids need guidance not 'figure it out.' Letting them suffer a little doesn't make them stronger it makes

you look unapproachable. Why not just rescue them? Why not just fix it? Why not make their life easier? You're acting like life has to be

hard for them to grow. They're kids. Kids shouldn't have to deal with natural consequences just so you can teach a lesson.

Why treat motherhood like a training camp? Do it for them. Don't make everything a 'lesson.' They'll learn eventually."

THE ANSWER

You think I'm letting them suffer. But what I am doing is refusing to handicap them."

"Let me tell you something every strong adult wishes someone had taught them sooner:

If you rescue a child every time they cry, you raise an adult who collapses every time life happens"

You say I should help? I DO help. But not by doing it *for* them. By teaching them they CAN do it. You think I'm being harsh because you only

see the moment. I see the future. I'm not raising kids. I'm raising future adults. Adults who will: pay bills, face heartbreak, solve problems, clean up their own mistakes, wake up early be disciplined, make decisions, survive disappointment, manage money protect their mental health,

and stand on their own two feet when the world does not care how "hard it feels." You say I should rescue them?

Christianity says it. Neuroscience says it. Life says it: "What you do for them, they never learn to do for themselves."

My job is not comfort. My job is formation. Not ease. Strength. Not sheltering. Preparing. Not rescuing. Raising.

When I don't run to find shoes, I am teaching independence. When I don't clean the mess they made, I am teaching accountability.

When I don't fix their friendships, I am teaching boundaries and discernment. When I stay quiet and let their brain turn on,

I am teaching critical thinking. Motherhood is not softness alone, it is strategy, wisdom, and spiritual endurance. You call it harsh?

I call it love with a backbone. Love that prepares them for a world that will NOT pause and say: "Aw, baby, let me fix it for you."

The world doesn't rescue. So neither do I. I guide. I steady. I support. But I do not prevent the lesson. God Himself placed in their path

to make them who they must become. If that makes me "harsh" to someone watching from the outside…. Then let them watch.

Because when my kids grow up: confident, capable, wise, responsible, mentally strong, emotionally stable, faith-rooted, and self-sufficient…

they'll realize something: Mami wasn't being cold. Mami was building soldiers with love so deep it looked like discipline.

And every one of them will say: "Mami wasn't lying."

Chapter 10

CUANDO TUVE QUE ACEPTAR QUE ESTUVE EQUIVICADA

(When I had to admit I was wrong)

I did not grow up around adults who admitted they were wrong. They doubled down. They got louder. They changed the story.
But they never said those words.

So when they came out of my mouth for the first time, it felt illegal. It happened over something small. That is how it always starts.

I had already decided I was right. I had the tone ready. The face. The explanation. I was tired. That mattered to me.
I had done more that day. That mattered to me. I was the adult. That mattered more. Or so I thought.

One of my kids called me out. Calm. No disrespect. No attitude. Just facts. "You said yes yesterday." I said no I did not.
They repeated it. Same words. Same calm. Still no

tone. Something in me flinched. Because I knew. I knew they were right.

And that is where the moment lives. Right there. The split second where you can lie to keep control or tell the truth and lose it. My chest got hot.
My pride stood up. My mouth almost defended something that was false. I felt the old reflex. Adults do not apologize. Mothers do not backtrack.
Authority does not bend.

That is how I was raised. But I looked at their face. Not scared. Not challenging. Just watching. Waiting to see who I was. So I swallowed it.
"I was wrong," I said. The room changed. Not dramatically. Not emotionally. Just quietly. They blinked. Once. Twice.
Then one of them said, "Oh." (Not relief. Not victory. Just information.). That is when it hit me.

I had been acting like admitting I was wrong would make me smaller.
It did the opposite. Because what I was really saying was

I pay attention
I remember my words

I am not afraid to correct myself
I do not need to pretend

That moment did more than a hundred lectures.

Later that night I thought about how many times I had been wrong in my life and refused to say it.
With men.
With family.
With myself.

Not because I did not know. But because saying it out loud felt like surrender. I confused honesty with weakness for a long time.
Street taught me something different.

On the street you earn respect by standing on your word. But you earn trust by fixing it when you miss. That is not soft. That is solid.

I started noticing how often I wanted to correct my kids when they corrected me. How fast my body reacted to being questioned.
How deep the programming went.

Nobody likes being wrong. But women especially get punished for it. If you admit fault you are told you are unstable.
If you stand firm you are told you are cold. If you

change your mind you are inconsistent.   So I stopped performing.

I decided I was not going to raise kids who were afraid of truth because of tone.   Or afraid of correcting authority because of ego.
The next time it happened I did not hesitate.   "You are right," I said. "I misunderstood."

No speech.
No explanation.
No defense.

They nodded and moved on.

That is power.

Because what they learned was not that I make mistakes.   They already knew that.   What they learned was that mistakes do not own you.
Silence does.

I am not interested in being seen as perfect.   Perfect is fragile.   Perfect shatters the first time life pushes back.
I am interested in being clear.

Clear enough to say I changed my mind.
Clear enough to admit I spoke too fast.
Clear enough to correct myself without humiliation.

That is not weakness.   That is authority without fear.

I notice the difference now.

When I say no, they listen.   Because they know it is real.   Not reactive.   Not ego.

When I say yes, they trust it.   Because I do not rewrite history to protect myself.   I did not lose respect that day.
I gained something heavier.   Credibility.   And the wild part is this. It made my house quieter.   Not silent.   Just stable.   Because when kids know
the truth will survive the room, they stop yelling to protect it.

I wish someone had shown me that earlier.

I spent years apologizing to the wrong people for things that were not mine.
And refusing to apologize when I actually should have.

Now I know the difference.

I do not apologize to be liked.
I do not apologize to smooth things over.
I apologize when I am wrong.

And when I am not.   I stand still.   That is the balance.   That is the lesson I did not inherit but chose anyway.

Mami was not lying.   I just had to unlearn what strength was supposed to look like.

Ecclesiastes 7:8

The end of a matter is better than its beginning, and patience is better than pride.

This is about restraint. About not reacting first. About letting the moment finish before ego steps in.

It directly mirrors you pausing instead of defending yourself

A PRAYER FOR PARENTS

God,
teach me the difference between authority and ego.
Help me notice when I am defending my pride instead of protecting my child.

Give me the courage to admit when I am wrong without feeling like I failed.
Slow my mouth when I want to justify.
Steady my body when I feel challenged.

Let my children see strength that does not need to overpower them.
Let my honesty make them feel safe, not confused.

Remind me that correction does not weaken leadership. It clarifies it.

Amen.

A PRAYER FOR TEENS AND CHILDREN

God,
help me trust my voice even when I am young.
Help me speak clearly without being afraid.

Teach me that adults can learn too.
That being wrong is not the end of respect.

When I make mistakes, help me fix them instead of hiding them.
When I am corrected, help me listen without shutting down.

Help me grow strong on the inside.
Amen.

NEUROSCIENCE INSIGHT FOR PARENTS

When a parent admits they are wrong, the child's nervous system relaxes.
Research shows that this reduces threat responses in the brain and increases trust and emotional regulation.

Children learn self correction not from lectures but from modeling.
When they see an adult pause, reassess, and repair, their brain learns that mistakes are safe to face.

This builds resilience, not fear.
Confidence, not compliance.

TEEN SIDE BAR

Adults do not always get it right.
That does not mean you are disrespectful for noticing.

There is a difference between being rude and being honest.
There is also a difference between standing up for yourself and trying to win.

You are allowed to say
You said something different before

I feel confused
Can we talk about it

Learning how to speak without attacking is a skill that will protect you for life.

REFLECTION QUESTIONS

For parents

When was the last time I knew I was wrong but defended myself anyway

What do I fear losing when I admit a mistake

Do my children feel safe correcting me

What kind of authority do I want them to remember

For Teens & children

Do I speak up or shut down when something feels unfair

Can I explain my feelings without yelling or blaming

Do I listen when I am corrected or do I immediately defend myself

What does respect look like when both people are learning

Chapter 11

LO QUE ME NEGUÉ Y LO QUE ME PUDO HABER COSTADO

(WHAT MY DENIAL ALMOST COST ME)

This is the part of parenting people do not admit because it sounds ugly when you say it out loud.

You can lose yourself without meaning to.

I hear parents say it all the time. "Vete pa ya." (Go over there). "Don't you get tired of talking." "I don't have time for this right now."

And the kid was not being bad. They were not asking for much. They just wanted to show something they were proud of. Sit close.

Be in the presence of the person they love the most. I catch myself watching these moments and wondering how they became so normal.

How did we get to a place where children asking for connection feels like an interruption. Where a child's voice feels louder than it is.

Where being needed by the smallest people in the room irritates us more than being needed by adults. That

question stayed with me.
Why does a parent push their child away so quickly but show patience to a partner. Why does overstimulation show up with kids but not
with grown people. What makes a child's need feel heavier than anyone else's. It is not because parents love their partners more. It is because
children need us without restraint. A spouse pauses. A child does not. A partner understands timing. A child trusts access. Children do not filter
their need through politeness or convenience. They come as they are. Often. Repeatedly. Without apology.

And when a parent is already depleted, that kind of need hits the nervous system differently. Adults trigger our patience. Children trigger our capacity.

That does not make parents cruel. It makes them overstimulated and under supported. Another truth people avoid saying is this.
Many parents give their best emotional regulation to adults because adults can leave.

Children cannot.

So the safest place for frustration becomes the child.

Not consciously.
Not maliciously.
But consistently.

Add exhaustion.
Add unprocessed resentment.
Add the loss of self no one talks about.

And suddenly a child's request feels like pressure instead of love.

That is the part we have to be brave enough to face.

Because children do not experience rejection as stress relief.
They experience it as absence.

They do not hear
I am overwhelmed.

They hear
You are too much.

That is why awareness matters.

Not perfection.
Not guilt.

Awareness.

Therefore, not because your kids take too much. Not because you love them wrong.

But because you keep postponing yourself and tell yourself it is temporary.

You stop resting because something always needs to be done.   You stop asking for help because explaining feels exhausting.
You stop naming what you want because it feels unrealistic.

You do not announce the denial.
You just adjust to it.

That is how it becomes normal.

I did not notice it happening at first.   I was still functioning.   Still showing up.   Still handling business.

That is the dangerous part.

I thought I was doing what strong parents do.
Holding it down.
Pushing through.
Making it work.

But strength without permission turns into erosion.

I was not angry.
I was numb in small places.

I was not unhappy.
I was unfinished.

One day one of my kids asked me something simple.

"What do you like doing?"

Not what do you do for us.
Not what are you responsible for.
Just what do you like?

I opened my mouth and reached for an answer that used to be there.

Nothing came.

That silence told me more than exhaustion ever did.

Because children do not learn adulthood from our speeches.   They learn it from what we allow ourselves to be.

If all they see is sacrifice with no joy, they learn that love means disappearance.   If all they see is endurance, they learn that adulthood
is something to survive.

That was not what I wanted to pass down.

So I started telling the truth in small ways.

I am tired.
I need space.
I enjoy this.
I do not enjoy that anymore.

No one felt abandoned.
No one suffered.

What changed was the tension I had been carrying quietly.

My kids stopped watching me like I might break.
They stopped adjusting themselves around my fatigue.

That part surprised me.

When parents deny themselves too deeply, kids feel responsible without being asked.
They become careful.
They become alert.

When a parent allows themselves to exist fully, kids relax.

I am not raising children to repay my sacrifice.
I am raising them to live without guilt for being alive.

That means letting them see me want things.
Letting them see me rest.
Letting them see me choose joy without apology.

Mami was not lying.
I just forgot that I was allowed to be included.

Ecclesiastes 4:6
**Better one handful with tranquility
than two handfuls with toil and chasing after the wind.**

This is not about doing less.   It is about knowing when enough has been reached.

A PRAYER FOR PARENTS

God,
help me tell the truth about my limits without shame.

Show me where I have confused self erasure with responsibility.
Teach me how to care for others without abandoning myself.

Let my children see a parent.
Not a machine.
Not a martyr.
A whole person.

Amen.

A PRAYER FOR TEENS AND CHILDREN

God,
help me understand that my parents are human.

Teach me that I am not responsible for their happiness.
Help me grow without carrying guilt that does not belong to me.

Let me learn how to take care of myself without fear.

Amen.

NEUROSCIENCE INSIGHT FOR PARENTS

When parents ignore their needs for long periods, the nervous system stays in survival mode.
This creates chronic tension even in calm environments.

Children sense this tension and often adapt by becoming overly responsible or emotionally cautious.

When parents model rest, desire, and fulfillment, it signals safety to the brain.
Safety allows connection.
Connection supports healthy development.

TEEN SIDE BAR READ THIS IF YOU ARE A TEEN

If your parent is tired all the time, it is not because of you.
You are not meant to carry their sacrifices.

You are allowed to grow without shrinking yourself.
A healthy family lets everyone take up space.

REFLECTION QUESTIONS

For Parents:

Where have I postponed myself without checking the cost?

Do I believe my needs matter only after everyone else is satisfied?

What do my children learn by watching how I treat myself?

What would change if I allowed myself to want again?

For Teens & Children:

Do I feel responsible for my parents emotions?

Can I enjoy my life without guilt?

What does taking care of myself look like right now?

What kind of adult do I want to become?

Chapter 12

BOUNDARIES: THE BEGINNER'S GUIDE TO RESPECT

Boundaries are weird. Because we grow up hearing things like: "*Aquí no hay puerta cerrá', que tú no pagas renta.*"

(There's no closed doors here, you don't pay rent.). Or the classic: "*Respeta pa' que te respeten.*"

But nobody ever TEACHES you how to respect yourself. They just expect you to magically know. Except it isn't. Respect is learned. Earned.

Boundaries are built. And if you don't teach them early? Life will teach them late. And harshly. Tonight… my house is a live demonstration.

THE YOUNGEST AND THE "NO EN MI CARA" RULE

She walks into my room like she owns shares in my oxygen. "Mami, look what I drew!" Beautiful. I say. But I'm working. And I already explained the rule: Don't interrupt when Mami is working unless it's an emergency or someone is literally bleeding. She knows this.

But kids have amnesia when they get excited. She busts through the space again, loud, heavy-footed, Humming a melody

I lift my hand. Palm open. Stop sign in nay language. "No en mi cara." (Not in my face.) She freezes. Stunned.

I lower my voice but sharpen the tone. "Mami is working. Your drawing is beautiful. But interrupting is disrespectful. Show me AFTER."

She swallows. Nods slowly. Walks away shoulders low head looking down.

"Okay…"

That's the thing about boundaries, kids get offended before they get educated. Their ego reacts before their heart understands. But minutes later,

she comes back and knocks. *Knocks*. We're making progress. It is repetition without punishment. And I will correct her again without

changing my tone. <—That's the hardest part for a parent, because if you really look at it…. Most get frustrated and will succumb to yelling)
That is what teaches.

The middle one tries to do the creep-walk into my room like a ninja with bad planning. "Where you going?" I ask without turning.

He jumps. "Uh… can I borrow your charger?" "No." I reply while looking at my screen. How'd you even see me?? You didn't even turn your

head to look at me…he jokes then continues to ask "Why?! You have, like…." I raise my eyebrow tilt my head and look at him.

"That's not a reason. That's entitlement." He blinks. Hard. "Ask properly," I say. He straightens his back. Tries again.

"Mami… may I please borrow your charger?" "Now THAT," I say, "is respect." Boundaries teach humility, they teach tone.

Boundaries teach "I'm not your little friend." He hands me the charger back later without being told.

(Which would of never happened if I'd just let him sneak it.) Another win.

THE OLDEST AND THE DOORWAY OF RESPECT

She's arguing with someone on FaceTime, rolling her eyes, waving her hands like a novela extra. She walks past me, heated.

I call her name. "Ven acá." (Come here.). She turns. I look into her eyes. "Your attitude?" I say softly. "Keep it with the person you're talking to,

not with me." Her energy shifts. She takes a breath. "Mami… I'm sorry." "I know," I say. "But I'm not your punching bag. Aquí hay respeto."

(There is respect here.) She nods.

That's the thing about boundaries, kids don't push them because they're bad. They push them because you're safe. But safety doesn't mean you

tolerate disrespect. Safety means you teach them to direct their fire responsibly.

THE MOTHER'S REALIZATION

Setting boundaries doesn't distance you from your kids. It teaches them how to love you correctly. Because one day…someone outside this house

will try to walk over them. Lie to them. Manipulate them. Use them. Break them. Drain them. And the only thing that will save them…

is the voice they heard at home: "No. Not like that. Not here. Not to me." Boundaries teach respect. Respect teaches identity.

Identity teaches strength. And THAT is how parents raise warriors.

2 Timothy 1:7
For God gave us a spirit not of fear
but of power love and self discipline.

Why this works
Boundaries require calm power and discipline, not fear or yelling.

PRAYER

"Father, Teach me to set boundaries without fear,

to say 'no' without guilt, and to honor the home You trusted me with.

Help my children learn respect through my example, not through pain.

Strengthen our voices, guide our tone, and let our home be a place of firm love

and sacred discipline.

Amén."

NEUROSCIENCE INSIGHT
WHY BOUNDARIES = RESPECT

Boundaries regulate the **nervous system**, reducing chaos

Clear rules activate the **prefrontal cortex**, improving decision-making

Kids learn emotional regulation through **predictable structure**

When parents say "no" consistently, it rewires the brain to expect consequences

Respect grows from **consistency**, not fear.

Boundaries teach SELF boundaries later in life

Translation:

A kid who learns respect at home becomes an adult who demands respect in life.

TEEN SIDEBAR
LISTEN UP

You think boundaries are control?

No. Boundaries are love with a backbone.

They're not meant to cage you, they're meant to **protect you**

from becoming someone you're not proud of.

And newsflash:

Your parents also have feelings. Respect isn't a suggestion; it's a requirement.

Practice saying: "My bad. "Let me rephrase that." "I didn't mean it like that."

Your whole life will improve.

REFLECTION QUESTIONS

For Parents:

What boundary do you break the most with your kids?

What boundary do THEY break the most with you?

Are your boundaries clear or emotional?

How can you model respect without yelling?

For Teens:

Which boundaries feel annoying but helpful?

How does tone affect your relationships at home?

What boundary do YOU need for yourself?

How can you show respect without feeling controlled?

Chapter 13

THE PARENT YOU NEEDED VS. THE PARENT YOU BECAME

Some nights, when the house is finally quiet and the last light flickers off like a tired eyelid, I sit alone in the living room with a cup of tea that goes

cold before I touch it. That's when the voices come, not evil ones, not frightening ones, but the voices of my past selves, visiting like old ghosts

checking if I finally understand them.

The little girl inside me curls up on the couch first. La nena que grew up faster than her bones should have. The one who learned to read

danger by smell, who learned to recognize footsteps by rhythm, who learned to hide bruises under long sleeves and silence under long breaths.

She stares at me with big eyes and asks: **"Where were you when I needed you?"**

And the truth slices clean: I wasn't here yet. I wasn't strong yet. I wasn't healed yet and I wasn't born yet.

Not THIS version of me. The version she needed didn't exist back then. And that is the tragedy AND the triumph of motherhood.

Because every scar I survived became a tool I use now to protect the children who depend on me.

THE MOTHER YOU NEEDED

I needed a mother who stayed. Who didn't explode. Who didn't break me to feel whole. Who didn't ignore me when I cried quietly in the kitchen

so I wouldn't get hit. Who didn't compare me, criticize me, use me, or forget me.

I needed protection, guidance, love, comfort, structure. I needed miracles more than toys. I needed affection more than holidays.

I needed safety more than rules. I needed presence more than perfection. I needed someone who looked at me and didn't see a burden or a curse or a responsibility too heavy to handle. I needed someone who saw me as a child. But instead, I got pain. Chaos. Confusion.

Loneliness. Fear. Secrets. Trauma. Silencio criminal. And yet, I survived. Not because someone carried me. But because I crawled.

Because I held my own broken heart together with stubborn hope.

This is what happens when the women raising you are still learning how to be women themselves. I was surrounded by female figures who loved
me the best way they knew how.

When the women around you are doing their best but do not know what to teach. But love without tools leaves gaps. I do not blame my mother.
She was a child trying to survive her own storm.

The truth is I was raised by women who were still growing up. Women who carried wounds they never had time to examine.

They stood in the role of mother without being taught how to mother. Not from cruelty. From inheritance.

So I learned instead. Late. Painfully. On my own. Like many of you women out there.

THE MOTHER YOU BECAME

Fast forward to now… Three kids. Three different storms. Three different needs. One mother. Me.

A mother who cooks with tears drying on her face because the day was long, but the love is longer.

A mother who disciplines even though she was raised with screams.

A mother who protects fiercely even though nobody protected her.

A mother who listens even when she was never listened to.

A mother who apologizes even though no adult ever apologized to her.

A mother who holds her children tightly even though she grew up unloved.

A mother who loves them loudly even though she grew up unspoken for.

A mother who gives them stability even though she built hers from ashes.

THIS is the moment I realized: **I became the mother I needed by refusing to repeat the mothers I had.**

That is generational warfare. That is ancestral rebellion. That is divine restoration. That is healing disguised as everyday motherhood.

Every novela has that scene where la protagonista finally faces her villain and tells her truth without shaking. For me, the villain isn't a person.

It's the old version of me who believed trauma was her destiny, who believed survival was enough, who believed she'd never be different.

Tonight, I face her. I look her dead in the eyes with my warrior stance, chin up, ceja levantá, (Lifted eyebrow)

and I say: "Gracias por sobrevivir… pero yo me encargo desde aquí." (It means: "Thank you for surviving… but I'll take it from here.")

That's the moment the chain breaks. That's when the novela theme song hits.

That's when the camera zooms in and the audience gasps.

That's when the girl I used to be finally rests.

THE TRUTH THAT TRANSFORMS

You don't become the mother you needed by wishing. You become her through choice.   Through boundaries. Through healing, discipline,

grace, fire, mistakes. And through trying again tomorrow.

Every day you choose:

"Mis hijos tendrán lo que yo no tuve." (My kids will have what Ive never had)

And every day God whispers:

"I trusted you with them because you were the one who would break the cycle."

"God is close to the brokenhearted

 and saves those who are crushed in spirit."

PSALM *34:18*

PRAYER

"Lord,

Thank You for using my wounds to create wisdom.

Thank You for the strength to become the mother I never had.

Heal the child inside me that still remembers the hurt,

and guide the woman I am now into patience, grace, and courage.

Help me raise my children with the love that once felt impossible.

Amén."

NEUROSCIENCE INSIGHT
HOW HEALING CHANGES PARENTING

Childhood trauma wires the brain for survival, not connection.

But healing creates **new neural pathways**, allowing emotional presence.

Parents who break cycles activate the **prefrontal cortex** (logic, empathy, patience).

Treating your children with kindness reprograms your own brain.

Healing is literally **biological transformation** passed down to the next generation.

Translation:

When you heal, your children inherit peace instead of trauma.

TEEN SIDEBAR

Your mom isn't strict because she's mean. She's protective because no one protected her.

Your mom doesn't yell because she hates you. She's fighting battles you've never seen.

Your mom loves you loudly because she grew up unheard.

Before you judge her, ask: **"What did life teach her before I even existed?"**

Your mom is not perfect. But she's healing for YOU.

REFLECTION QUESTIONS

For Parents:

What part of your childhood shaped the parent you became?

Which habits are you breaking for your children's sake?

What would the younger you say

if she saw the mother you are now?

What new boundary or habit will you create to protect healing?

For Teens:

What's one thing you understand about your parent now?

How has your parent changed from the stories they've told you?

What does "respect" mean to you now?

How can you support peace in your home?

Chapter 14

RAISING LEADERS,

Some people raise children. Some people raise adults. But a few of us… **we raise leaders.**

And not leaders because we're perfect. We raise leaders because we had **no choice** but to become leaders ourselves.

Nadie me lo contó. Yo lo viví. (No one told me, I lived it) Raising three kids alone after losing all their fathers, with grief beating on my door daily,

with bills crawling up my spine, with trauma trying to choke me in my sleep. **And STILL… I got up. Still… I pushed. Still… I built.**

No miracle check in the mail. Just hustle. Faith. Strategy.

And the conviction that my kids would NOT become grown adults with toddler mentalities.

I've heard a saying:

"Si quieres criar un líder, prepárate pa' criar carácter." (If you want to raise a leader, prepare to raise character.)

Y eso mi amor…duele. (It's the hardest thing you could ever do)

The youngest…She used to explode like a mini-volcano anger, impulsive choices, crying, yelling.

I didn't baby her. I didn't pacify her rage. I didn't say, "It's okay, mami, scream all you want."

No.

I sat next to her and said: "Este mundo no perdona berrinches. ("This world does not forgive tantrums.")

"Pero sí respeta a quien se controla." (But does respect he/she who controls themselves)

The world doesn't reward chaos but it rewards people who master themselves.

She learned breathing. She learned pausing. She learned ownership.

Now? She apologizes on her own. She checks herself. She leads with emotional intelligence…not tantrums.

That's leadership.

The middle child: Responsibility builds back bone

A leader doesn't wait to be told. A leader anticipates. So when he left messes, forgot chores, slacked off, or acted lazy…

I didn't yell or beat them like my ancestors did. I didn't bribe and I didn't clean behind him. I stepped aside. And let Life teach him:

No discipline = no reward. No follow-through = no trust. No responsibility = no freedom.

He learned real quick that **Work first, fun later, Integrity is doing the right thing unasked**

A man who can't manage a room can't manage a future.

One day he told me: "Mami… I feel better when things are done, clear minded"

I said: "That's because you're becoming a man, not a grown boy."

The oldest: Social Leadership is knowing your value

Her lesson did not come from heartbreak. It came from watching.

She was invited into a group chat that moved fast. Too fast. Jokes that crossed lines. Plans made without thinking.

Opinions repeated because they sounded popular.

She did not speak right away. She read. She noticed who talked the most and who followed.

Who changed their tone depending on who was watching.

Someone tagged her and said…Say something you always quiet.

She looked at me and asked..Do I have to answer?

I said no.

You do not owe access just because someone invites you.

She stayed silent.

Later one of the girls messaged her privately. Why you acting better than everyone?

She did not rush to explain. She did not soften herself.

She answered calmly. I am not acting better. I just do not like the way this feels. That was it.

No apology. No over explaining. No performance.

The chat kept moving without her. Louder. Messier.

She stayed where she was. What she learned was quiet but permanent.

Not everyone deserves access. Loyalty is a privilege. Love is not a strategy. Respect is non negotiable.

Her intuition was not drama. It was information.

Leadership is not volume. It is restraint. Leaders do not chase validation. They set the tone.

Leaders do not shrink to belong. They belong to themselves first.

Leadership requires discernment. Most people fail at life because they fail at choosing people.

Her intuition is divine, not drama. Leaders don't follow the crowd. **Leaders lead.**

THE MOTHER'S REALIZATION: LEADERS ARE BUILT IN THE FIRE

Parents who depend on government aid for generations end up passing down survival, not leadership.

Parents who live in perpetual collapse emotionally, financially, mentally raise kids who collapse too.

But parents who get up? Parents who self-regulate? Parents who seek God first and strategy second?

Parents who face the world with courage? Those parents raise titans.

Leadership is caught and taught. And if you want leaders in your house, YOU must lead first.

It's not about money. It's not about education. It's not always about resources. It's about MINDSET.

And mindset…. that's free.

"Train up a child in the way he should go, and when he is old, he will not depart from it."
PROVERBS *22:6*

PRAYER

"Lord,

Give me the strength to raise children of character, not comfort.

Give them courage to stand firm, wisdom to lead with love,

discipline to honor their gifts, and integrity that cannot be bought or shaken.

Bless the single mothers raising armies with empty hands and full hearts.

Let our children walk in purpose because we walked in faith.

Amén."

PRAYER FOR TEENS AND KIDS

God,
help me trust myself even when I am quiet.

Teach me that I do not have to follow the crowd to belong.
Help me notice when something feels wrong and give me the courage to step back.

Show me that my worth does not change based on who accepts me.
Help me choose friends who respect me and walk away from what does not.

Give me strength to stand alone if I need to.
And wisdom to know when silence is power.

Amen.

NEUROSCIENCE INSIGHT
HOW LEADERSHIP DEVELOPS IN CHILDREN

Leadership is not genetic. It's BUILT through:

Emotional regulation (calm under pressure)

Executive function (planning, decision-making)

Resilience circuits (overcoming struggle)

Mirror neurons (copying YOU)

Autonomy (doing things without being rescued)

Praise for effort, not entitlement.

Kids raised with structure AND love develop:

- ✓ Higher confidence
- ✓ Better problem-solving
- ✓ Stronger mental flexibility
- ✓ Lifelong discipline
- ✓ Emotional maturity
- ✓ Leadership instincts

Parents who break generational dependency literally rewire their children's brain chemistry toward success.

TEEN SIDEBAR READ THIS

A leader is not someone who bosses people around.

A leader is someone who:

Handles their anger. Thinks before reacting. Takes responsibility

Stands alone when needed. Works when no one is watching

Protects their family. Protects their peace

Chooses wisely. Speaks with purpose

Listens twice as much as they talk

Being a leader starts with ONE question:

"Would I follow me?"

REFLECTION QUESTIONS

For Parents:

What leadership traits do you want your children to embody?

Are YOU modeling those traits daily?

Which habits from your upbringing are you breaking intentionally?

What responsibilities can you give your children this week to strengthen discipline?

For Teens:

What makes someone a leader in your eyes?

What decision have you made recently that showed maturity?

What is one habit you can change to improve your future?

How can you hold yourself accountable this week?

Chapter 15

LET ME THROW THIS IN HERE

Some people raise children. Some raise adults. And some of us? We raise WARRIORS because life didn't give us the luxury

of raising soft, confused, helpless little décor pieces who can't survive a Tuesday. You want to know why I raise leaders?

Because this world don't play fair. It doesn't care if you're tired, sad, overwhelmed, or "just a kid."

Life will throw bills, heartbreak, consequences, responsibilities, trauma, and opportunities at them. WITHOUT WARNING. And MY kids?

They're gonna be ready. Not allergic to effort. Not dependent on rescuers. Not fragile like vegan glass.

Let me break it down

1. "They're just kids!" EXACTLY. That's why I start NOW.

People act like childhood is a bubble bath. No, mi amor.

Childhood is the *training ground* for adulthood. A kid who:

✓ throws tantrums at 12 will throw tantrums in relationships at 22+.

✓ avoids responsibility at 10 will avoid accountability at 30+.

✓ relies on others to save them as kids becomes the adult who blames everyone else for their mess.

I'm not raising liabilities. I'm raising LEGACY.

2. "Why don't you rescue them?" Because I'm not raising professional victims.

Wanna know the problem with society? Everybody wants to be rescued. Nobody wants to be responsible. Not my house.

If they mess up? They fix it. If they forget something? They learn. If they ignore advice? Life steps in with the *chancleta invisible del destino. (Look it up)*

CONSEQUENCE > COMFORT.

Because comfort raises weak minds. Consequences raise strong ones.

3. "But you're too tough!" Tough? BABY, LIFE IS TOUGH. I'm the SOFT LOVING version.

Life will:

- repossess your car
- reject your application
- snatch your job
- expose fake friends
- crush your heart
- laugh at your excuses
- and bill you for the damage

I'm giving them the gentle version of pain. LIFE will give them the savage kind.

You're welcome.

4. "Kids need to be free!" …..Yes, free… and FUNCTIONAL.

Without discipline? Freedom becomes chaos.

Without guidance? Freedom becomes self-destruction.

Without responsibility? Freedom becomes entitlement.

I'm not raising kids who grow up thinking the world owes them anything.

I'm raising kids who BUILD their own softness through character, wisdom, work ethic, faith, and self-respect.

5. I don't raise consumers. I raise PRODUCERS.

Anyone can spoil a kid. It takes a REAL MOTHER to build a mind that can survive long-term.

Spoiled kids grow into adults that crumble when life stops handing them things. My kids? They'll still be standing.

Because I taught them how to use their hands, their heart, and their head before the world demanded it.

That's not to say I don't spoil them, I just don't overdo it.

6. You know what feels bad?

Watching your grown child:
- fold under pressure
- choose the wrong partner

- fail because of laziness
- get manipulated
- fall into debt
- depend on the system
- lose themselves
- repeat generational patterns you fought to break

THAT hurts.

Teaching them NOW?

That's love. That's protection.   That's legacy.

7. "But they're gonna say you were strict!"… LET THEM.!   Leaders always thank you later.

Kids complain now.   Adults understand later. My kids will grow up and say: "Mami didn't play.   But Mami prepared me."

THE FINAL MIC DROP:

I'm not raising "kids." I'm raising:

- future CEOs
- future mothers/fathers
- future professionals

- future protectors
- future decision-makers
- future leaders
- future adults who won't crumble

I'm raising a generation that breaks cycles not repeats them. If that intimidates you? That's a sign you weren't raised like this.

Si no te gusta mi estilo (If you don't like my style, just pray for yours)…ponte a orar por los tuyos. Porque yo?

I'm building an army God entrusted to ME.

Chapter 16

OH ALSO…. for the mamas and papas.

If you're reading this last page, it means you made it through the fire with me.   You cried, you laughed, you got mad,

you rolled your eyes and maybe…just maybe…you saw yourself in my children…or in me

and you saw your mother or the mother you needed in me.   So sit with me for one last moment.   Not as an author and reader.

Not as parent and child.   But as two souls who survived something that should've broken us.

Let me tell you something straight. **You were never meant to raise kids in perfection.   You were meant to raise them in truth.**

And truth is messy.   Truth is loud.   Truth has stretch marks and bills and trauma and early mornings where coffee is a prayer and late nights

where silence becomes therapy.   Truth builds leaders.   Not entitlement.   Not excuses.   Not shortcuts.

Every child you raise will one day be an adult walking through the world carrying either your brokenness…or your healing.

And look at you!! YOU CHOSE HEALING. Even when it hurt. Even when you were tired. Even when you didn't have examples.

Even when the enemy whispered you weren't enough. But God whispered louder: **"Sigue. I'm with you."** So you kept going.

And that's what makes a mother unstoppable. Let these final words stay with you like a blessing on your forehead and a shield over your home:

You are not raising perfect humans.

You are raising prepared ones.

You are raising grounded, grateful, gritty warriors.

You are raising future leaders, not grown children.

You are raising destiny.

And if nobody told you today if nobody hugged you right if nobody gave you credit for carrying entire worlds in your hands

let ME be the one to say it: **I'm proud of you. God is proud of you. And your future self is screaming "thank you" from the mountaintop.**

Now go… hold your babies, fix your crown, and keep leading that home with the same fire, softness, discipline, and love

that got you all this way. **Porque tú, mami or papi… you were never ordinary. You were chosen.**

And every chapter of this book proves exactly that.

THE REBUTTAL and answer

Why end the book like THAT?   That's too dramatic

Ahhh…*mira qué lindo.*

Another person who thinks this is a Hallmark movie and not real life.

Let me explain something with the sharpness of an abuela saying, "Cállate y escucha." ("Shut up and listen") You call it dramatic.

I call it **honest**. You call it intense. I call it what survival feels like. You call it "too much."   I call it **everything nobody told us growing up**.

This last page wasn't written for fragile people who melt when truth gets hot. It was written for parents who have walked barefoot through hell

with kids holding onto their shirt and STILL managed to smile in the morning like nothing was burning behind them.   Let me break it down:

1. "Why so emotional?"

Because parenthood IS emotional.

If you want sterile, robotic advice, go read a pamphlet.

But if you want the REAL:

the exhaustion,

the beauty,

the spiritual battle,

the trauma,

the breakthroughs,

the nights you cried alone,

the mornings you rose anyway

THIS is the language it comes in. Raw. Sacred. Messy. Powerful. If that makes you uncomfortable, WELCOME. Growth always does.

2. "Why talk about God?"

Because without God I wouldn't have made it past chapter one. Let's be very clear: Science explains the brain.

God transforms the soul. And parenting requires BOTH. If you want to raise leaders without the One who gives them purpose, good luck.

But in this home? We mix faith with strategy because that's how you build children who don't fall apart when life gets spiritual,

financial, emotional, or mental.

3. "Why mention single mothers?"

Because single mothers are the backbone of entire countries. And society loves to use them but not honor them.

So yes, I said it: We raise leaders because we HAD TO. We grow spines out of trauma. We grow wisdom out of chaos.

We grow strength out of abandonment. You don't have to like that. But you WILL respect it.

4. "Why the fire? Why the intensity?"

Because passive parenting creates passive adults. You want soft? Go hug a pillow.

You want leadership? You get fire. You get accountability. You get the truth people avoid. You get the blueprint nobody gave us.

This isn't a fairy tale. This is a manual for generational change. And generational change does not whisper. It ROARS.

5. "Why say you're proud of the reader?"

Because too many parents have NEVER heard that sentence in their whole life. Some people grew up with:

"No sirves para nada." (You're a good for nothing). "You're too much." "You're failing." "You're ruining everything."

And they carried those wounds into adulthood, into parenthood, into their homes. This book is written to BREAK that curse.

And I will scream it loud if I have to:

YOU ARE DOING A GOOD JOB
 EVEN WHEN IT DOESN'T FEEL LIKE IT.

If someone can't handle that? That says more about them than about this book.

6. "The last page feels like a speech."

GOOD. It was meant to. Because THE END of a book and or chapter should feel like the BEGINNING of a new version of you.

You're not supposed to close it and feel nothing. You're supposed to close it and say: "wow. I'm built different."

"My kids deserve this version of me." "I'm ready."

If my words shook something awake in you… mission accomplished.

People who complain about the tone are people who've never had to carry a family on their back.

People who say "dramatic" are people who never stepped into their healing.

People who say "too much" are people who've never had to be EVERYTHING when nobody else showed up.

This chapter wasn't written for them. It was written for YOU. The chosen ones. The cycle-breakers. The parents raising leaders with empty hands,

a full he

Chapter 17

DIOS TAMBIEN EDUCA…(GOD EDUCATES…) JUST NOT THE WAY YOU THINK

There are moments in life when you swear God is ignoring you. When nothing makes sense. When every door slams. When every plan crumbles.

When every step forward feels like ten backwards. But hear me, corazón…**God may be silent but He's never still.**

And when you're a mother? Ay bendito…. God teaches you in ways that look NOTHING like the cute little devotionals you see on Instagram.

Sometimes God speaks through blessings. Sometimes God speaks through breakthroughs. But MOST of the time? God teaches through:

Inconveniences

interruptions

delays

consequences

pain

and the people who swear they know more than you

Because Dios es amor, sí… Pero Dios también es **maestro**. Y fuego consumidor. "God is love, yes… but God is also a teacher. And a consuming fire."

And the lessons hit differently when you're raising teenagers, kids, children, young adults…

THE LESSON YOU DIDN'T SIGN UP FOR

That week, everything in my house felt upside down. My youngest was snapping like a firecracker.

My middle child was in his "¿por qué yo?" (Why not) phase. And my oldest? Was dealing with social identity, school, future….

I prayed the way every single mother prays: **"God, give me strength… pero dame templanza también, porque sin eso, voy presa."**

("But give me temperance too, because without it, I'll end up in jail)

***SIDE NOTE FOR EVERYONE ***

(If you ask God for patience You're asking for the ability to **endure** something without reacting.

It's about waiting, holding back frustration, staying calm while something continues…

Instead ask God for temperance, you're asking for **self mastery**. Control over impulses. Restraint when emotion spikes.
Wisdom over reaction. Temperance helps you **govern yourself**, not just endure others.

Patience is waiting.
Temperance is restraint.

Patience keeps peace.
Temperance keeps you free.)

God, in his time, hilarious as always answered with a situation instead of a solution, because that's how He teaches.

You want patience?   He sends chaos.

You want wisdom?   He sends confusion.

You want peace?   He sends noise.

You want growth?   He sends struggle.

 God doesn't hand you the fruit. He sends you the seed.

And then He watches how you water it, nourish it to growth

WHEN NOTHING BROKE BUT EVERYTHING SHIFTED

The oldest and the room that went quiet. She came home talking fast about a group project. Too many details. Too much justification.

I listened without interrupting. Everyone had an idea. Everyone wanted credit. Everyone talked.

Then she said one sentence that slowed her down. "And nobody actually decided anything."

That was the collapse. Not drama. Not betrayal. Just noise with no direction.

She realized something in real time. Being smart does not make you a leader. Being loud does not make you right.

Later that week she told me she stopped explaining herself in the group. She started asking one question instead.

"What are we actually doing."

The room changed.

Not because she forced it. Because clarity has weight. That's when it made sense to her. Leadership is not being impressive.

It is being steady when others spiral. Nothing fell apart. But her understanding clicked into place.

The middle child

He forgot his lunch. I noticed before he left. I said nothing. At school he got hungry. Not starving. Just uncomfortable.

When he got home he told me. I nodded. No lecture. No apology.

The next morning he packed it himself. Carefully. Double checked.

That was the the moment he realized someone was not going to rush behind her fixing things. Responsibility did not feel cruel.

It felt clarifying. She learned this quietly. Comfort disappears. Awareness replaces it. And that awareness stays.

The youngest and the question that stopped the noise

She was frustrated over nothing specific. Everything felt wrong. The toy annoyed her. The sound bothered her. The room felt unfair.

I almost corrected the behavior. Instead I asked one question. "Are you tired or overwhelmed." She just looked at me.

"I dont know," she said. The moment she realized feelings are not enemies. They are signals.

We sat. No fixing. No distractions. Later she said she felt better. Not because the problem went away. But because someone helped her name it. That was the sense. Emotions calm down when they are understood.

WHAT I LEARNED WATCHING IT ALL

None of this looked like a breakdown. No yelling. No speeches. No rescue scenes.

But every child crossed a line they will never uncross. They learned that confusion clears. That hunger teaches. That emotions have language.

I did not grow for them. I did not interrupt the process. I stayed present and let reality finish the sentence.

That's when I understood something I had been fighting. Collapse does not always mean damage. Sometimes it means alignment.

And when it finally makes sense, it does so quietly. Like truth usually does.

"Whom the Lord loves He corrects."
PROVERBS *3:12*

PRAYER

Señor… help me trust Your timing when my children struggle.

Teach me when to speak, when to guide,

and when to step aside so You can do the teaching.

Give them resilience, give them understanding,

give them a heart that feels You even when they don't see You.

And give me the strength to watch them grow even through pain.

Amen.

PRAYER FOR TEENS/CHILDREN

God,
help me understand my feelings when I do not have the words.

When things feel confusing or hard, help me pause instead of panicking.

Teach me that mistakes are part of learning and that I am still loved while I figure things out.

Help me listen, grow, and try again.

Amen.

NEUROSCIENCE INSIGHT

When children experience mild stress, natural consequences, problem-solving struggles, emotional processing

their brains activate the **prefrontal cortex**, the area responsible for:

✓ decision-making

✓ emotional regulation

✓ impulse control

✓ empathy

✓ maturity

Overprotecting your child can delay the development of these systems.

Translation:

If you rescue them too much, you raise them weaker than life requires.

TEEN SIDE BAR (REAL TALK)

Hey, corazón… Listen carefully:

When Mami steps back, it's not because she doesn't love you.

It's because she knows you're stronger than you act.

Life won't always rescue you. So she's teaching you how to stand now

before life knocks harder.

You're becoming an adult…and adults have to **think**, not just react.

REFLECTION QUESTIONS

What lesson is God trying to teach YOU right now as a parent?

Where do you intervene too quickly with your children?

What fears stop you from letting your kids struggle?

Which of your childhood wounds still affect your parenting?

What would trusting God more in your parenting look like?

Chapter 18

THE RESPECT THEY SWORE THEY NEVER NEEDED

Respect is funny. Kids act like they invented it. Teens act like it's optional. Adults pretend it's automatic.

But Respect is survival. Respect is culture. Respect is inherited and passed down like family jewelry, except sharper.

And the craziest part? The ones who need the MOST respect… are always the ones who swear they "don't need it from NOBODY."

Ay, bendito.

Let me tell you about the week respect finally hit home in my house not with lectures, not with yelling, not with threats…

but with reality, consequences, and a twist only life could write.

THE DISHES INCIDENT OF THE CENTURY

It started with the middle child. he was standing in the kitchen, scratching the top of his head

lip curled looking at TWO plates in the sink like they were asking him to climb El Yunque (Puerto Rico's National Forest) barefoot.

"Mami, WHY CAN'T THEY DO IT? WHY ALWAYS ME?"

And for the first time in years, I didn't argue. I didn't explain. I didn't negotiate.

I simply turned around, grabbed a chair, and sat. he froze. "Mami… what are you doing?"

"Watching," I said. "Watching what?" "Watching how long it takes for life to teach you what you think you already know."

His face went blank. Because tweens and teens understand everything…until they try doing everything.

He washed the plates, dried them and put them away. No applause.

No thank you. No parade. And I could SEE that realization hit him: Respect isn't about chores. Respect is about community.

Family. Responsibility. And fairness true fairness not the version kids invent. Sometimes respect enters through the kitchen sink.

THE YOUNGEST AND THE CHARGER OF DOOM

The youngest exploded over a charger again but this time, the disrespect wasn't the yelling…

it was the disconnection. You can't teach respect to a nervous system in fight-or-flight. You have to reach the CHILD under the chaos.

So instead of correcting the tone, I held the wrist gently and said:

"breathe." With some resistance. Tried to pull away, eyes were wild.

But then… she inhaled. Deep. Slow. And as the shoulders dropped, something happened:

She finally HEARD me. Because respect isn't just behavior it's regulation. It's connection. It's being able to see the person in front of you.

Respect starts with **self-awareness** and sometimes they discover it mid-meltdown.

THE OLDEST: THE BETRAYAL THAT OPENED HER EYES

When her friend betrayed her, twisted her words, spread lies, and made her the villain… The old her would've fought fire with fire.

But something changed. She sat on the edge of the bed and said: "Mami… I didn't even argue.

I just walked away. I'm not wasting my peace."

And mamá… I nearly cried. Not because she didn't fight.

But because she finally understood something MOST adults don't:

Respect is energy conservation. Respect is knowing who deserves your voice. And who deserves your silence.

Not everyone gets access to you.

Not everyone gets reaction from you.

Not everyone gets to pull you out of character.

This was her graduation day. No cap and gown. Just wisdom.

AND THEN CAME MY LESSON

"Respect begins with you. Not them." Not in the bossy way. Not in the "I'm your mother" way.

But in the: "I model the emotional maturity I want you to imitate" way.

And I felt that deeply. Because being a single mother, being a mom period means being:

the disciplinarian

the leader

the nurturer

the structure

the comfort

the provider

the safe space

the everything

…ALL AT ONCE.

If my kids forget respect, it's rarely personal it's developmental. They're learning how to be humans with human brains and human emotions

in a household where mom carries the weight of everything. Respect isn't taught by force. It's taught by consistency.

And that day, we all learned something about each other.

"Do to others as you would have them do to you."
LUKE 6:31

PRAYER

Lord, teach my children to honor themselves,

honor their home, and honor the people who love them most.

Help me model the respect I want to see in them,

and give us patience, clarity, and peace during moments of tension.

Make our house a place where respect grows naturally,

not through fear but through understanding.

Amen.

NEUROSCIENCE INSIGHT

Respect is tied to three developing brain regions in teens:

✓ **Prefrontal Cortex** (judgment, impulse control)

✓ **Anterior Cingulate Cortex** (empathy + emotional correction)

✓ **Amygdala** (fight-or-flight reactions)

When they feel:

unsafe

misunderstood

overwhelmed

overstimulated

…their brain defaults to survival mode, not respect mode.

Stable parents create stable brains. Stable brains create respectful children.

TWEEN/TEEN SIDE BAR

Respect isn't about "being told what to do."

It's about:

being fair

being grateful

being responsible

being aware

being in control of YOU

When you disrespect your parent, you don't look powerful.

You look unprepared. And trust me…

Life checks unprepared people HARD.

This chapter is your warning AND your blessing.

REFLECTION QUESTIONS

What triggers disrespect in your home?

How do YOU model respect (or disrespect) without noticing?

Which child struggles with boundaries the most? Why?

How can you create small daily rituals that reinforce respect?

What part of respect do YOU wish you learned earlier?

Chapter 19

THE CHILD YOU WERE VS. THE PARENT YOU BECAME

There's a moment in every parent's life... un momento tan fuerte, tan inesperado... where you realize your entire childhood is standing right in front

of you, but not as memories. As your children. Their reactions mirror yours. Their fears echo yours.

Their anger resembles someone you used to be. Their silence...their confusion...their disrespect... their tenderness... their strength...

It all comes from a version of you you didn't choose but had to survive. And THAT realization? Hits deeper than therapy.

Deeper than prayer. Deeper than any novela plot twist. Because suddenly, you're not just raising kids **you're reparenting yourself.**

THE CHILD YOU WERE

You were a child navigating chaos. A home divided between faith or fear. Survival and silence.

Maybe you were raised by a mother who was a pastor…. Or a family who practiced witchcraft in the shadows

Or an athiest family. Maybe.. a house full of unspoken wars. Siblings who were more like soldiers. A brother who protected you even

though he was younger. Adults who ignored, dismissed, or punished your pain. Rooms filled with secrets. Doors that never locked.

Nights that never felt safe. And the worst part? **Nobody came for you.** Nobody rescued you from the touches that weren't right…

the beatings that were too hard…

the threats that silenced your voice…

the torture disguised as discipline…

the manipulation disguised as love…

the abandonment that shaped your bones…

the responsibility that felt like punishment…

the prayers that didn't match the violence…

And yet…despite ALL OF IT…

You became a mother who fights for her kids the way no one ever fought for you.

THE PARENT YOU BECAME

You became:

the safe space

the protector

the stability

the voice of truth

the structure

the softness

the strength

the prayer warrior

the therapist

the teacher

the comfort

the discipline

the legacy

the guide

the storm-calmer

the peace-maker

the cycle-breaker

You became the parent you needed.

But here's the part nobody talks about:

Being a cycle-breaker is exhausting.

Being a generational architect is heavy.

Being the first one to do it right feels lonely.

Sometimes you discipline your kids with the fear of becoming your parents.

Sometimes you overprotect them because nobody protected you.

Sometimes you get overwhelmed by their emotions because nobody ever taught you yours.

Sometimes you lose your patience because that's how you were taught to respond.

Sometimes you see your younger self in them and it hurts more than you admit.

But MOST of the time? You love them in ways you CHOSE. Not ways you inherited.

And that's what makes you powerful.

THE MOMENT THEY SEE YOU

One day maybe sooner, maybe later your children will realize you weren't harsh…

you were healing. You weren't strict because you wanted to be mean…

you were protecting. You weren't "overreacting"… you were breaking curses they don't understand yet.

They will realize you loved them LOUDER than anyone ever loved you.

That you mothered them with scars instead of manuals, with pain instead of guidance, with trauma instead of tenderness…

And STILL gave them a childhood better than your own. That's strength. That's grace. That's spiritual leadership. That's motherhood.

Not every woman who becomes a mother can master those.

"The Lord is near to the brokenhearted

 and saves the crushed in spirit."

PSALM*34:18*

PRAYER

God…

thank You for staying beside me through every wound that shaped me and every lesson I had to learn alone. Give me the wisdom to parent from healing,

not from fear. The strength to love without repeating the past.

The patience to raise my children with grace

even when I am tired. And help me forgive the child I used to be,

so she can finally rest.

Amen.

NEUROSCIENCE INSIGHT

Trauma doesn't disappear, it reappears in parenting.

Your nervous system remembers danger, reacts to tone, overcorrects misreads emotion, gets triggered, floods with stress,

goes into survival or shuts down. NOT because you're a bad parent… but because you were not taught emotional regulation as a child.

Here's the science you NEVER got as a kid:

✓ The brain rewires through consistency

✓ Healing is emotional, not just physical

✓ You can reparent yourself WHILE raising your kids

✓ Your new patterns become their normal

✓ You break generational cycles one regulated moment at a time

You are not your parents , your brain is changing every time you choose differently.

TEEN SIDE BAR

Listen up… Your mom became who she is WITHOUT the help you're getting now.

She didn't have a safe space. She didn't have emotional tools. She didn't have the support system you take for granted.

She didn't have a guide. So when she corrects you, guides you, or disciplines you…

She's not being strict. She's loving you the way she WISHES she was loved.

Show her grace. Show her effort. Show her respect.

Not because she's perfect but because she's healing while raising you.

REFLECTION QUESTIONS

What parts of your childhood still influence your parenting?

What did you need as a child that you now give your kids?

Where do you overcorrect because of past wounds?

Which parenting patterns are you consciously breaking?

How can you reparent YOURSELF while guiding your children?

Chapter 20

MAMI NUNCA MINTIO….TU NO ESCUCHASTE (MOM NEVER LIED YOU JUST DIDN'T LISTEN)

There's a moment in every child's life and a moment in every mother's life where the truth you've been screaming in silence finally lands.

Not because you said it louder. Not because you repeated it a hundred times. Not because you explained it perfectly. But because life…

finally caught up with their ears.

THE DAY THE TRUTH GREW LEGS

It happened on a Wednesday. My oldest walked into my room slowly like someone approaching a judge.

Can I ask you something?" She asked

"Were you…were you right? About everything?"

I didn't move. I didn't gasp. But inside? My spirit did the merengue.

Because THIS was the moment I'd prayed for… not so I could say "I told you so," but because I wanted her to SEE what I had been trying to protect her from all along.

Mothers have this magical, supernatural gift: **ver lo que tú no ves** (seeing what you don't see) before it even happens.

Call it intuition. Call it discernment. Call it trauma-lasered perception. Call it God speaking a little louder to mothers.

But the truth is this: Moms read people faster than therapists. Especially the quiet ones, the smiling ones,, the hidden manipulators.

And teens? They always believe the best in everyone even when the signs are dancing reggaetón in front of them.

So when my middle child came to me angry at a friend, I remembered… I warned her weeks ago.

And she brushed it off with "Mami, you're overthinking. That's just how she is. You don't understand."

Ah yes. The anthem of adolescence. But now she stood in the doorway looking like: "Mami… you saw it before I did."

And I wanted to tell her:

"Porque yo veo con experiencia. Tú ves con inocencia."

("Because I see with experience. You see with innocence.")

THE LITTLE ONE LEARNS THE HARD WAY

The youngest was the toughest. Fire. Passion. Angel one second, hurricane the next. She didn't believe me when I said:

"Not everyone who laughs with you is laughing *for* you." Until one day one tiny, petty moment a girl she trusted twisted her words,

mocked her, and left her crying in the bathroom. She came home destroyed. And when she curled into my chest, I didn't say a word.

Because she didn't need an "I told you so." She needed a mother who understood this pain intimately from childhood.

From betrayal. From the cruelty of girls who pretend to be kind. And under her breath she whispered:

"Mami… you were right."

THE MOMENT YOU WANT TO GLOAT BUT CAN'T

Let me tell you something: Cuando un hijo te dice "tenías razón"…(When your child tell you "You were right"

You earn a secret stripe in motherhood. But you don't celebrate. You don't flaunt it. You don't rub it in. You just breathe… and thank God.

Because the goal was never to be right the goal was to **guide.** To **protect.** To **prepare.** To **break the cycles your parents didn't break for you.**

You see, **Teens don't actually hate advice. They just hate accountability.**

And moms? We don't want control. We want clarity. We want safety. We want maturity.

We want self-awareness. We want them to avoid pain we had to swim through as kids.

But it hits different when life teaches the lesson. Because life is patient…but also petty.

THE REAL REVELATION

This chapter is not about "being right."

It's about the moment your child realizes:

you weren't trying to limit them

you were trying to protect them

you weren't being extra

you were being aware

you weren't assuming

you were discerning

you weren't judging their friends

you were seeing spirits and intentions they couldn't see

you weren't overthinking

you were spiritually alert

you weren't crazy

you were experienced

you weren't strict

you were safeguarding the future they can't imagine yet.

Mami nunca mintió. Ellos simplemente no estaban listos para entender.

("Mami never lied. They just weren't ready to understand."). But when they finally do? It changes your relationship forever.

JEREMIAH 7:24

"But they did not listen or pay attention.

They followed the stubborn inclinations of their own hearts."

PRAYER

Lord…

Thank You for every moment where truth catches up to understanding.

Help my children SEE what I've tried to teach,

and help me guide them with patience, clarity, and love.

Give them discernment, protect their hearts,

and let them recognize wisdom even when it comes softly

through a mother's warning.

Amen.

PRAYER FOR TEENS AND CHILDREN

God,
slow me down before I dismiss what I do not like hearing.

When someone warns me,
help me stop arguing long enough to listen.

Keep me from learning the hard way
when the truth was already in front of me.

Give me wisdom early
so I do not have to earn it through regret.

Amen.

NEUROSCIENCE INSIGHT

The teenage brain is wired for: reward-seeking, peer approval, social risk, emotional immediacy

blindness to manipulation, temporary trust over long-term safety.   Parents don't "know more" because they're older.

They know more because their **prefrontal cortex is fully developed.**

A mom's intuition is a combination of:

✓ experience

✓ trauma-history awareness

✓ micro-expression reading

✓ subconscious pattern recognition

- ✓ emotional intelligence
- ✓ spiritual discernment

So when a mother says:

"Ese no me gusta," ("That person doesn't inspire trust")

it's not superstition. It's neurobiology and discernment teaming up.

TEEN SIDE BAR

LISTEN

Your mom isn't psychic.

She's practiced.

She's been hurt.

She's been betrayed.

She's been manipulated.

She's been naïve.

She's been you.

She's not trying to control you.

She's trying to SAVE you from a pain she remembers too well.

Don't wait for the lesson to become scars when you can learn it through her voice instead.

REFLECTION QUESTIONS

When did you ignore your intuition and regret it later?

What warnings did your mother give you that turned out to be true?

In what areas are your kids repeating your mistakes?

Where can you use your experience to protect them better?

What truth are YOU refusing to hear right now?

Chapter 21

TU NO ERES UN BILLETE DE CIEN PA CAERLE BIEN A TO' EL MUNDO

(YOU JUST AIN'T A $100 TO BE LIKED BY EVERYONE)

There's a moment in life usually right after betrayal, heartbreak, rejection, or some fake friend switching up where you finally realize:

NOT EVERYBODY IS SUPPOSED TO LIKE ME."

And when that realization hits you for real, not pretend. Your entire soul unlocks like a cellphone face ID. Because listen….

You are NOT a hundred-dollar bill. You are NOT made for universal approval. You are made for purpose, not popularity.

But try telling that to a teenager. Especially a Latina teenager with big emotions, big presence, and big dreams.

Ay, Señor. (Oh Lord)

THE NOVELA OF APPROVAL SEEKING

It started with something small: A video. A comment. A group chat. A joke that wasn't funny.

My oldest daughter walked in looking defeated. And she said the phrase every mother knows too well:

"Mami… why don't they like me? I didn't do anything."

Ah…. the heartbreak of being disliked for simply existing. I pulled her close and said: "Corazón… entiende algo (understand this) now, not later:

People who are intimidated by you will always pretend they don't like you." She blinked at me. "But why? I'm nice."

"Honey… BEING NICE ISN'T THE PROBLEM."
I smiled.

"Your confidence is.

Your light is.

Your potential.

Your intuition.

Your presence.

Your discipline.

Your standards are.

Your self-respect is."

People don't dislike *you*.   They dislike how they feel about themselves when you walk into the room.   And THAT, my love, is psychological truth.

WHEN YOU STOP TRYING TO IMPRESS EVERYBODY…

I told her a truth that took ME 30 years to learn:

"You are not meant to be

digestible,

neutral,

harmless,

comfortable,

or convenient."

"You are meant to be YOU.   And YOU is not for everybody."

In fact… if everybody likes you… you're living too small.

Backing down.

Shrinking.

Dimmed.

Muted.

One thing about a Boricua mother or any good mother?

We don't raise kids who shrink. We raise kids who shine…aunque les moleste a los ciegos. (Even if it bothers the blind)

The middle child learned the hard way too.

He tries to make friends through kindness. And sometimes? People take kindness as weakness. Classic rookie mistake.

One day he came home saying: "Mami… I was so nice to her and she still treated me bad."

I leaned back like a novela protagonist ready to deliver a line:

"Mi amor… kindness is your character. Their reaction is their character. Don't confuse the two."

"A diamond doesn't become fake just because someone with cheap taste can't appreciate it."

He laughed. Because some truths crack the ego, but heal the soul.

But…

My baby with the fiery personality? She had the opposite problem.   She didn't care if people liked her.

She cared too much about fighting anyone who DIDN'T.   Ay Dios mío… One day she said:

"I don't care if they don't like me.   I'll FIGHT THEM."

And I had to breathe before answering.   Because she meant it.

So I sat her down: "Mamá… don't give your power away through fists.

Give your power through presence.   Some people dislike you because they see your strength and feel their own weakness."

"Let them feel it.   You don't have to swing to prove anything."   And for the first time…she nodded.

Like she knew her strength was bigger than her reaction.

THE LESSON FOR MOTHERS

We want our kids to be liked. It makes school easier. Friendships easier. Family gatherings easier. Life easier.

But easy doesn't build leaders. Being disliked sometimes is the first sign your child is walking in purpose.

And for us? The mothers? We also have to accept the truth:

You are not here to be liked.

You are here to be effective.

Impactful.

Aligned.

Whole.

Unshakeable.

Obedient to God, not people.

A leader, not a people-pleaser.

Approval is nice. Purpose is better

"If the world hates you, remember it hated Me first."

JOHN *15:18*

PRAYER

God...

Help my children understand their worth even when others don't.

Let them walk in confidence, not comparison; in purpose, not popularity.

Protect their hearts from envy, their minds from insecurity,

and their spirits from seeking validation from those who cannot see their value.

Teach them to stand strong in rooms where they feel misunderstood...

and remind them they were created to shine, not to be approved.

Amen.

PRAYER FOR CHILDREN

God,
help me know I am special even when others do not notice.

Remind me that I do not have to be the loudest or the fastest to matter.

Protect my heart when I feel left out
and help me remember that I am loved just as I am.

Teach me to be kind to myself
and brave enough to be who You made me to be.

Amen.

PRAYER FOR TWEENS

God,
help me believe in myself when I start comparing.

When I feel unsure or awkward,
remind me that growing takes time.

Protect my heart from trying to fit in at the cost of who I am.
Help me choose confidence over approval
and honesty over pretending.

Teach me that my worth does not change
based on likes, friends, or opinions.

Amen.

PRAYER FOR TEENS

God,
help me stand firm when I feel misunderstood.

Let me walk with confidence instead of chasing validation.

Protect my mind from comparison
and my heart from shrinking to belong.

When others cannot see my value,
help me remember who I am and whose I am.

Give me strength to be myself
even when it would be easier to blend in.

Amen.

NEUROSCIENCE INSIGHT

The human brain is wired for belonging especially in childhood and adolescence.

BUT…

The brain also matures through:

✓ social friction

✓ rejection

✓ emotional resilience

✓ boundary-setting

✓ identity formation

✓ self-concept development

Studies show:

Teens who learn early that not everyone will like them develop stronger self-esteem and lower anxiety in adulthood.

Being universally liked is NOT a sign of strength. It's a sign of **self-abandonment.**

TEEN SIDE BAR

If someone doesn't like you, it doesn't mean you're wrong.

It might mean you're too real for them. You don't need fans.

You need standards. You don't need to fit in.

You need to grow. You don't need approval.

You need direction. And trust me…

The people who matter will find you

without you shrinking to be seen.

REFLECTION QUESTIONS

Where in your life did YOU seek approval growing up?

Which child struggles most with needing to feel liked?

Which one struggles with NOT caring enough?

How can you teach them that confidence and softness can co-exist?

What part of YOU still wants to be liked and how can you release it?

Chapter 22

OUR LEGACY STARTS WHERE THE EXCUSES DIE

There is a moment in every mother's life where you stop surviving…and you start building. A moment where your past stops being your prison and becomes your blueprint. A moment where your wounds stop bleeding and begin teaching. A moment where you realize:

Legacy doesn't begin when life gets easier. It begins when YOU get disciplined.

People think legacy is money. Or inheritance. Or properties. Or degrees. But mi amor… legacy is decisions. Legacy is character.

Legacy is faith in action. Legacy is choosing what your parents didn't. Legacy is doing what no one taught you.

Legacy begins the moment your excuses die.

THE DAY EVERYTHING SHIFTED

The kids were arguing in the living room. Bills on the table.

A to-do list longer than a pile of laundry looking like it wanted to talk back.

And I stood there thinking: "I have two choices: keep surviving…or start transforming." And right then?

I realized what God had been trying to show me all along… Excuses come from fear. Legacy comes from courage.

And courage doesn't feel good. It feels like nausea, shaking, praying, or crying, fumbling, trial-and-error, late nights, early mornings,

overthinking, restarting… But courage is obedience. And obedience creates destiny.

THE EXCUSES WE HOLD AND THE CHAINS THEY BECOME

Let's be honest…We tell ourselves:

"I'm too tired."

"I'm too busy."

"They don't listen."

"I have no help."

"I'm doing it all alone."

"My childhood messed me up."

"No one taught me this."

"I don't know where to start."

But the truth is:

Excuses are grief wearing a mask.   Excuses are trauma buying time.   Excuses are fear pretending to be logic.

And when you're raising kids alone like I did, after losing every one of their fathers to tragedy, life, and death

no one tells you: Your life won't pause for you to heal. Your kids won't wait for you to figure it out.   Your responsibilities won't shrink just because

you're hurting.   You either sink… or you swim.

And most of us women?   We swim with thunder in our chest.

THE MOMENT MY EXCUSES DIED

I sat at the kitchen table, looking at my children, three souls depending on MY decisions, MY emotional stability, MY faith,

MY consistency. And I said this sentence out loud:

"I'm not raising dependents. I'm raising LEGENDS."

And legends cannot be built on shortcuts.

Not on fear.

Not on survival mode.

Not on "mañana lo hago." (I'll do it tomorrow

Not on generational bad habits.

Not on chaos disguised as normal.

So I killed every excuse with one prayer:

"God…

I don't know how, but I'm willing." And He moved. Not magically… but methodically.

He opened doors I didn't even knock on. He cleared paths I didn't know I needed.

He removed people I was too attached to. He lit fires under me I couldn't ignore.

And He showed me: **Legacy isn't built when you're ready. Legacy is built when you're willing.**

When you believe in it so much you bring it into reality. Thats how it works. That's how it worked for the bleeding woman in the books

Matthew, Mark and Luke of the Bible. She just touched Jesus clothing and she was cured..

Not because he had super powers but because she truly believed.

LEGACY IS DAILY WORK

Not once in a lifetime. Not when you feel motivated. Not when things calm down.

Daily. Consistent. Uncomfortable.

Legacy means:

✓ Setting standards

✓ Setting boundaries

✓ Not negotiating your worth

✓ Not tolerating disrespect

✓ Making your kids responsible

✓ Teaching discipline through action

- ✓ Letting consequences shape them
- ✓ Praying even when tired
- ✓ Working even when drained
- ✓ Healing even when busy
- ✓ Growing even when scared

Legacy is not DNA. Legacy is decision.

One night my oldest said: "Mami…you don't get tired?"

And I laughed. Not because it was funny, but because it was REAL.

"Of course I get tired," I said. "All the time. But I refuse to let my exhaustion raise you. My standards will."

She got quiet. And then she whispered: "Mami… I want to be like you someday." And right there…

THAT SINGLE SENTENCE… became the moment I knew…. My legacy had already begun.

"Write the vision; make it plain."
HABAKKUK *2:2*

PRAYER

Lord…

Help me build a legacy rooted in You, not in fear.

Help me raise children that honor their purpose, not their excuses.

Give me strength when I have none, discipline when I feel weak,

and clarity when everything feels heavy.

Let my children inherit wisdom, faith, courage, and truth

not trauma, fear, or silence.

Amen.

PRAYER FOR TEENS AND CHILDREN

Lord,
help me grow into who You created me to be,
not who fear tries to make me.

Give me courage to choose what is right
even when it is not easy.
Teach me to learn from my past
without being trapped in it.

Let me inherit wisdom instead of wounds,
truth instead of silence,
and strength instead of fear.

Help me build a future that is better,
stronger,
and freer than what came before me.

Amen.

NEUROSCIENCE INSIGHT

The brain rewires through:

✓ repetition

✓ structure

✓ consistent behavior

✓ habit reinforcement

✓ emotional modeling

Kids don't always learn legacy from what you SAY. They learn it from what they SEE.

Your discipline literally becomes the architecture of their developing brain.

Consistency = security

Standards = identity

Boundaries = emotional intelligence

Responsibility = maturity

Faith = resilience

Legacy begins in their neural pathways long before it becomes their adulthood.

TEEN SIDE BAR
LISTEN UP

Your mom is not being "dramatic." She's building your future.

She's protecting your destiny. She's not doing "too much." She's doing EVERYTHING

she wishes someone did for her. Honor that. Respect that. Walk in that.

Your excuses end here.

Your legacy begins now.

REFLECTION QUESTIONS

What excuses are holding YOU back?

What legacy are you currently building consciously or unconsciously?

What habits or behaviors need to die for your children to grow?

What standard do you need to raise today?

What does "legacy" mean for your family specificall

Chapter 23

GENERATIONAL CURSES VS GENERATIONAL CHOICES

(Lo Que Heredas… y Lo Que DECIDES Romper)
What you inherit and what you decide to break

There are wounds you didn't ask for. Ghosts you never met but still fight in your sleep. Patterns you swore you'd never repeat, until one day

you open your mouth, say something to your kid, and hear your mother's voice come out. Not her tone. Not her accent. Her *wounds*. Her words

And in that moment… your chest tightens. Your throat burns. Your heart whispers:

"Dios mío… I'm becoming what hurt me."

But breathe, This is not shame. This is revelation. This is the moment every cycle breaker faces:

when you realize generational curses aren't spooky witchcraft, they're inherited *reactions*. Unhealed stories. Survival reflexes passed down like

family heirlooms. Some families pass down jewelry. Some pass down trauma responses. And yet…here you are. Reading a book that your

parents never had. Learning lessons your bloodline never learned. Fighting demons they never dared to name.

THE TRUTH:

Generational trauma is not your fault. But breaking it IS your responsibility.

Because curses don't continue through magic…they continue through *patterns*.

And what you don't heal? Your children will inherit.

What IS a Generational Curse?

✓ A curse is a scream your abuela swallowed

✓ A fear your mother called "normal"

✓ A wound your father hid behind silence

✓ A pattern your family repeated so much it became culture

✓ A lie you were taught so young you thought it was love

A curse is not a spell.

It's a story that was never corrected.   A temper no one learned to manage.   A secret no one wanted to expose.

A burden everyone's back got used to carrying.   And when you raise kids alone?   Those curses get LOUD.

LOUD like a car alarm at 3 a.m.   LOUD like a pressure cooker screaming from the kitchen.
LOUD like speakers clipping because they're turned too high.

"If I don't break this… my kids will live this."

THE SCIENCE OF GENERATIONAL TRAUMA

Neuroscience says:

Your kids don't just inherit your eye color, they inherit your **stress responses**.

Children absorb:

- Your tone
- Your coping skills
- Your silence
- Your triggers
- Your emotional language
- Your "this is how we survive" rules

The brain mirrors what it sees. Not what you *wish* they learned.

When you yell instead of feel, their brain imprints:

"Intensity = power."

When you shut down instead of talk, their brain learns:

"Disconnect to stay safe."

When you over function for everyone, their brain records:

"Exhaustion = love."

Kids don't copy your intentions. They copy your patterns.

And THIS… THIS is where generational curses get exposed.

THE GOD SIDE OF IT:

Cycles break where truth begins. God doesn't break curses with magic words. He breaks curses with **decisions**.

With the mother who chooses honesty over hiding. With the father who chooses accountability over denial.

With the parent who says: **"It ends with me."**

That's why YOU are chosen. Not because you're perfect. But because you're *willing*.

Willing to heal.

Willing to reflect.

Willing to unlearn.

Willing to do the uncomfortable thing your parents never did.

EXAMPLES:

Where Curses End and Choices Begin

1. YOUR ANGER

Inherited curse:

Impulsivity, yelling, reacting without thinking.

Your generational CHOICE:

Teaching your kids emotional regulation instead of fear-based obedience.

2. YOUR POVERTY MINDSET

Inherited curse:

Survive, not thrive.

Hustle from desperation, not strategy.

Your generational CHOICE:

Raising kids who understand money, discipline, and stewardship not "pray for a miracle and hope the check clears."

3. YOUR RELATIONSHIPS

Inherited curse:

Settling for emotionally unavailable people because "algo es algo." (Something is something and it's better than nothing)

Your generational CHOICE:

Showing your kids what boundaries look like so they never confuse attention with love.

4. YOUR SELF-SILENCING

Inherited curse:

Swallowing pain because parents back then called it "fortaleza." (Strength)

Your generational CHOICE:

Teaching your kids vocabulary for their feelings so they don't grow up emotionally illiterate.

WHY YOU ARE THE CYCLE BREAKER

(even if you don't feel like one)

Because you QUESTION patterns your family defended.

Because you RECOGNIZE behaviors that once felt normal.

Because you CHOOSE differently even when you're scared.

Because you WANT better, even if you never saw it.

Because you've become the mother you needed, the father you never had,

the healer your bloodline prayed for without realizing YOU were the answer.

THE PAINFUL PART NO ONE TELLS YOU

Breaking generational curses feels like betrayal.

You will feel guilty.

You will feel alone.

You will feel like "maybe I'm being dramatic."

You will feel your ancestors tugging at your sleeve saying:

"Pero así siempre se ha hecho."

(But this is how we've always done it.)

Ignore them.   Because your children's future is louder than your past.

THE BEAUTIFUL PART THEY DON'T TALK ABOUT EITHER

Your kids will grow.

Stronger

Kinder.

More stable.

More aware.

More emotionally intelligent.

More connected to God.

More prepared for adulthood than you EVER were at their age.

They will become the proof that your suffering wasn't wasted.   Your healing will become their inheritance.

You will break a curse and your kids won't even know one existed.

They won't know:
- How close you were to giving up
- How much you had to unlearn
- How many nights you cried
- How much restraint it took not to repeat history

They won't know… because you refused to pass it on.

And THAT right there? is leadership at its highest form.

PRAYER

"Lord,

Make me brave enough to confront the curses

my family normalized.

Give me strength to choose healing

even when pain feels familiar.

Protect my children from wounds I've survived.

Let my decisions today

be the freedom they walk in tomorrow.

Amen."

NEUROSCIENCE INSIGHT

WHEN YOU HEAL, THEIR BRAIN CHANGES TOO

Healing your trauma reshapes THEIR brain wiring.
Literally.

✓ Your calm rewires their nervous system

✓ Your boundaries create their confidence

✓ Your self-control becomes their foundation

✓ Your healing becomes their blueprint

Generational curses break not through talk but through **consistency + regulation + accountability.**

REFLECTION QUESTIONS

For Parents:

What emotional reflex from your childhood still shows up in your parenting?

What cycle are you actively breaking?

What did your parents call "normal" that you now recognize as harmful?

What pattern do you want your children to NEVER inherit?

For Teens:

What behavior in your family feels "normal" but uncomfortable?

What pattern scares you about your future?

What wound are you ready to heal so you don't pass it down?

Chapter 24

RAISING KIDS IN A DIGITAL WORLD

There's a new monster in the house and it doesn't hide in closets, under beds, or in the hallway at night. It glows. It buzzes. It pings.

It vibrates. It knows your child better than their own mother does sometimes. Screens aren't evil.

But the addiction they create? Eso sí. That's the real demon. The digital world is raising kids faster than parents can say

"dame ese iPad ahorita mismo." ("Give me the iPad right now")

Tonight, my house is quiet. Not peaceful quiet, artificial quiet

brought to you by blue light, TikTok, and 30-second brain-numbing loops.

My youngest is in the corner, scrolling the same meme eight times. My middle one is "doing homework" with YouTube open.

My oldest is staring at her phone like she's waiting for God's text message.   And me? I'm watching them all with the suspicion of a novela villain

who already knows the plot twist:

The phone is raising them while they think I'm being dramatic.

THE SCARY TRUTH NO ONE TELLS YOU

Sometimes Your kid isn't lazy or disrespectful or "unfocused." Your kid is overstimulated.

Their dopamine baseline is fried.   Their nervous system is sprinting even when they're sitting still.

Screens trained their brain to crave constant stimulation and you wonder why they "can't sit through a conversation"

or "forget everything you say."   Your child's brain is drowning.   And the water is entertainment.

THE YOUNGEST: ATTENTION SPAN IN CRISIS

She sits on the couch scrolling… scrolling… scrolling… Her thumb moves faster than her brain.

I say her name once. Nothing. Twice. Nothing. By the fourth time, I'm ready to summon the chancleta.

Finally she snaps up.

"WHAT?!"

I look at her…eyes wide open.

"¿Qué tú aprendiste en los últimos diez minutos?" (What'd you learn the last ten minutes?)

She freezes. Eyes blinking. Mouth open. "uhhh…nothing."

Exactly.

TikTok isn't entertainment. It's hypnosis. She isn't addicted to her screen, she's addicted to dopamine bursts so tiny and constant that real

life feels boring by comparison. I sit next to her and say mamita…you need a break."

She sighs the dramatic sigh kids make, all loud coming from her chest. But she listens. And that's step one.

You may ask…ok..how about if they don't listen? Here's a couple thing you may do…

1. Give warnings with choices, 5 minute warning then 2 minute warning. Provide choices to increase compliance.

Do you want to put the phone on the charger or the drawer?

2. Immediately redirect them to something stimulating… a new activity.

(Yes, even if it means you have to take out of your time to spend time with them)

3. Enforce Predetermined Consequences; Use "loss of privilege" language. follow through example… if the phone isn't put away..

they lose it for the rest of the day. And then you will still have to redirect them to do something else. (Have different activities set up…

like card games, family game time for an hour or two every night,

ensuring you yourself follow through as an example putting your phone away as well)

4. You could threaten, yell scream, send them to their room. Like our parent and their parents and their parents parents etc…

But let's be serious what is that going to do? but create animosity between the parent and child.

It is difficult as parents to be present more than what our parents were.

It takes a lot of effort and elbow grease. But you chose to have this child.. were done creating dysfunctional families.

Standing in the doorway, I know he noticed me there….The middle child…He's doing homework. Or pretending.

Every five seconds he switches tabs.   Like his brain is a radio he can't tune.   "Mami, I'm trying!" "No," I say.   "You're overstimulated.

Your brain is on Colombian coffee strength right now and you haven't even had water." He groans. I point at the invisible watch on my wrist.

"Ten minutes. One task. No switching. When you're done, break." He complains.   He rolls his eyes.

He acts like I asked him to build a pyramid with his bare hands.   But after the ten minutes?

"Wow… I actually finished something."   He says…

Because his brain didn't need motivation it needed less noise.

The oldest. She walks into my room with her phone clutched like a lifeline. "Mami… I don't know what's wrong with me. I feel sad.

Like something is wrong… but nothing happened." I tell her "Let me see your phone. I'll give it right back."

I take her phone and what do I see…"You fed your brain 800 strangers' emotions in two hours," I say. "That's not sadness.

That's emotional overload." She gasps. And tells me no way!! So I give her an example

Because nobody told her this: When you scroll past drama, breakups, glow-ups, trauma dumps… your brain absorbs ALL of it.

You're not meant to feel the whole world in one night. I open my arms. "Come. Your nervous system needs real human connection, not WiFi."

She scoffs, rolls her eyes then just melts into me like someone unplugging for the first time.

Screens aren't the enemy.

Lack of discipline is.

Lack **of boundaries** is.

Lack **of emotional literacy** is.

Lack of **parental backbone** is.

Technology isn't going anywhere. The world our kids are entering will require digital fluency AND self-control.

So my job is not to confiscate the device. My job is to teach them to dominate it. To raise kids who scroll with purpose, not kids who drown in noise.

HOW TO BUILD DISCIPLINE IN A DIGITAL WORLD WITHOUT BEING A DRILL SERGEANT

1. DIGITAL DETOX WINDOWS

Not punishment. Just protection.

30 minutes with no screens will feel like rehab at first but becomes freedom later.

2. USE SCREENS INTENTIONALLY

Entertainment? Okay. Education? Amazing.

Mindless doom-scrolling? Nah. That's how brains rot.

3. LET THEM BE BORED

Boredom builds creativity.   Screens kill it.

Bored children become imaginative adults.

Overstimulated children become dependent ones.

4. SCRIPT THE EMOTIONAL EXIT

Teach them to pause and breathe before switching apps. This retrains dopamine tolerance.

5. LEAD BY EXAMPLE

If you're scrolling all day your kids are studying YOU not your rules.

THE REAL REASON THIS MATTERS

Because overstimulated kids become anxious adults.

Because dopamine-addicted teens become unfocused parents.

Because kids who can't unplug grow into adults who can't connect.

Discipline in a tech world is not about control.   It's about FREEDOM.

Because the child who learns to master their attention masters their future.

PRAYER

"Lord,

Protect my children's minds from overstimulation.

Give them clarity in a world built for distraction.

Teach them to seek purpose over noise

and peace over chaos.

Help me model self-control

so they can build it too.

Amen."

NEUROSCIENCE INSIGHT

THE DIGITAL BRAIN IS A DIFFERENT BRAIN

✓ Every notification spikes dopamine

✓ Fast-content rewires attention span

✓ Overstimulation causes irritability, mood swings, anxiety

✓ Emotional exhaustion comes from consuming too many people's lives

✓ Teens mistake dopamine crashes for depression

✓ The brain NEEDS stillness to reset

Screens aren't destroying children.   Overuse is.

Moderation builds discipline.   Discipline builds leaders.

TEEN SIDEBAR

Your phone is not the enemy. Your boredom isn't killing you.

Your brain is asking you to breathe.

If you ever feel:

- annoyed for no reason
- sad out of nowhere
- overwhelmed
- tired but wired
- unable to focus

It's not your personality.

It's your brain begging for space.

Try unplugging for 10 minutes.

You'll be surprised how human you actually are.

Chapter 25

"When Your Child Has a Strong Personality… and You Have to Raise Them Alone."

There's a special kind of child God sends to the strongest parents. Not the quiet ones. Not the easy ones. Not the "yes, Mami or Papi" ones.

No….

The ones with fire in their chest, opinions in their blood, and leadership written in their DNA…

but stuck inside a developing brain that still eats cereal like a toddler.

These kids don't "talk back."

They *stand up*.

They don't just "challenge authority."

They *test structure*.

They don't just "misbehave."

They *practice leadership* on the person they trust most, YOU.

And the WORST part? They act different with the other parent. Different with grandma.

Different at school. Why?

Because YOU are the safest place to test their power.

THE HARDEST PART:
TWO PARENTING STYLES

You already know how this story goes:

One parent:

✓ structure

✓ discipline

✓ boundaries

✓ accountability

✓ follow-through

The other parent:

✗ excuses

✗ inconsistency

- ✗ "déjalo, no es para tanto" (Is not that serious)
- ✗ letting everything slide
- ✗ sugary words and no backbone

And who does that child unload on?

YOU.

The strong parent.

The stable parent.

The consistent parent.

The parent who actually parents.

And it's not fair.   And it's exhausting.   And some nights you stare at the ceiling like:

"Señor, ¿tú estás seguro que este era mi asignación?" God did you give me the right assignment?

But listen to me:

Strong-willed children *steal softness* from the permissive parent… and **show ALL their fire** to the parent they know won't break.

If the other parent is inconsistent, weak, absent, careless, irresponsible, or immature… guess who becomes the emotional battlefield?

YOU.

THE TRUTH YOU MUST SWALLOW EVEN IF IT HURTS

A strong-willed child raised by **two inconsistent parents** becomes lost.

A strong-willed child raised by **one inconsistent parent** becomes divided.

A strong-willed child raised by **one strong parent** may become a leader.

And you… may be the ONLY stability they have.

Not because you're perfect. Not because you want to do it alone.

But because you refuse to raise a child who becomes a grown-up with the emotional maturity of a potato.

THEIR "BAD BEHAVIOR" ISN'T BAD, IT'S UNTAMED LEADERSHIP

Listen:

Kids with fire aren't always trying to destroy your house. They're trying to understand their power.

And if you don't teach them discipline… the world will teach them consequences.

If you don't teach them boundaries… the world will teach them rejection.

If you don't teach them respect… the world will teach them humiliation.

If you don't teach them self-control… the world will teach them captivity.

You're not the villain. You're the trainer.

WHAT MAKES THESE KIDS DIFFERENT

These children Question EVERYTHING

Want reasons, not rules, don't care about tone, only logic

Some have zero patience for hypocrisy, some are the learned hypocrisy

Some see through manipulation instantly and can't be guilted, bribed, or forced

Only follow strength, not weakness

And that's exactly why YOU are the chosen parent.

Not the soft one.   Not the passive one.   Not the permissive one.

YOU

the disciplined one,

the backbone,

the "no es no,"

the "I love you, but try me and you'll learn today,"

the mother/father warrior with God on speed dial.

THE BREAKING POINT NOBODY TALKS ABOUT

When two parenting styles exist:

You become the enforcer The other parent becomes the escape

You become the "bad guy".   The other becomes "fun"

You carry 90% of the emotional labor.   They get 100% of the affection

It's unfair.   It's enraging.   It's heartbreaking.

But here's the plot twist:

Some kids gravitate back to the parent with structure…

because structure = safety.

Even if they don't understand that yet.

THE TURNING POINT

One day after all the yelling, crying, grounding, exhaustion.

That same strong-willed child will come to you and say:

"Mami/Papi… you were right."

Because leaders don't grow where everything is easy.
Leaders grow where expectations exist.

YOUR ROLE IN RAISING A LEADER LIKE THIS

You must:

✓ Stay consistent

- ✓ Stay calm
- ✓ Stay unmoved
- ✓ Stay anchored
- ✓ Stay disciplined
- ✓ Stay firm but loving
- ✓ Stay grounded in God

Because a strong-willed child needs a parent who doesn't break when they push.

YOU are that parent.

"Those who sow with tears will reap with joy."
PSALM 126:5

You're not crying because you're weak.

You're crying because raising a leader is holy work.

PRAYER

"Lord,

Give me the strength to guide a child whose fire You placed on purpose.

Show me how to mold their will without breaking their spirit.

Help me stand firm even when the other parent is inconsistent.

Cover this child with wisdom, direction, and humility.

May their strength become leadership and not rebellion.

Amen."

NEUROSCIENCE INSIGHT

STRONG PERSONALITY KIDS = HIGH EXECUTIVE POTENTIAL

Research shows they have:

Higher dopamine drive

Stronger reward-seeking

Faster pattern recognition

Dominant prefrontal traits (leadership circuits)

Resistance to authority unless it feels "logical" or "earned"

Translation:

They're not "bad."

They're wired for leadership

but leadership without discipline becomes destruction.

They need a parent who provides structure, not softness.

SIDEBAR FOR TEENS

Before you roll your eyes…

Here's the truth:

Your strong personality is a gift.

But if you don't learn self-control… the world will mistake your strength for disrespect.

Your mom or dad aren't trying to "boss you around."

They're trying to teach you how to lead without burning your life down.

If they're hard on you… it's because your potential is bigger than your feelings.

REFLECTION QUESTIONS

For Parents:

Which of my child's behaviors are actually leadership traits in disguise?

Where am I being too soft because I feel guilty?

Where am I being too harsh because I feel alone?

How can I become the unshakeable parent my strong-willed child needs?

For Teens/Tween/Kids

Do I want to be powerful or impulsive?

Do I react because I'm right or because I'm triggered?

What kind of leader do I want to be?

What parts of my personality need discipline?

BONUS CHAPTER #1:

WHEN THE OTHER PARENT UNDERMINES YOUR DISCIPLINE

(La parte que nadie quiere admitir… pero TODO el mundo sufre.)

There is a very specific rage only single parents know: The rage of disciplining your child with love, structure, and boundaries…

just for the other parent to undo EVERYTHING in 10 minutes.

You say "No phone tonight."

They say "Here, take my phone."

You say "Your room needs to be clean before you go out."

They say "Don't worry about that, let them have fun."

You say "We don't talk to adults like that."

They say "Déjalo, no es para tanto." ("It isn't that serious")

You say: "This is a consequence."

They say: "You're too strict."

You're raising a future leader.

They're raising a future problem.

And who gets blamed?

YOU.

THE TRUTH NO ONE WANTS TO SAY OUT LOUD

When a parent undermines you, they are not being "nice." They are raising an undisciplined adult with a child's mindset and an adult's consequences.

There is NOTHING more dangerous than that. Kids turn manipulative not because they're evil but because they learn two systems:

One parent reinforces reality.

One parent reinforces fantasy.

Guess who becomes the enemy?

The parent who's actually parenting.

The strict parent is "mean" now. But becomes the blueprint for success.

YOU are the blueprint.

THE STRATEGY ONLY STRONG PARENTS USE

You cannot teach the other parent maturity.

You cannot teach them consistency.

You cannot teach them structure.

You can only:

✓ Stay firm

✓ Stay calm

✓ Stay consistent

✓ Stay grounded in your rules

✓ Not compete

✓ Not collapse

✓ Not change your structure because theirs is weak

Because a child with ONE stable parent is STILL more grounded than a child with two unstable ones.

You are building a mental backbone not a people pleaser. You are raising a leader not a liability.

And when the world hits them? They won't run to the "fun parent." They'll run to the one who prepared them.

YOU.

BONUS CHAPTER #2:

HOW KIDS PLAY ONE PARENT AGAINST THE OTHER

These kids are smart. Like "CIA-level manipulation in a 12-year-old body" smart.

They know: One parent says no. One parent says yes. So they test.

They twist your words.

They leave out details.

They exaggerate.

They pretend innocence.

They cry strategically.

They weaponize softness.

They act confused.

They fabricate timelines.

They fake misunderstanding.

Not because they're evil.

Because they're learning power. But here's where YOU take back control

THE 3 THINGS THAT STOP MANIPULATION INSTANTLY

1. "Unified Front With Yourself"

If the other parent won't unite with you, YOU become the unity.

Translation:

Your rules stay your rules no matter who says what.

"Mami said no." Still no.

"Papi said yes." Still no.

"Grandma said I could. Still no.

You cannot control them.

You can only control your household.

And consistency kills manipulation.

2. No Emotional Negotiations

Kids don't manipulate logic. They manipulate EMOTION.

So the secret is simple:

Be the parent who doesn't fold when the crying starts.

You don't yell. You don't chase. You don't debate.

You say your rule once.   Then hold the line quietly.

Silence cuts through manipulation sharper than any speech.

3. The "Consequences Travel" Rule

If they break a rule in your house, the consequence follows them everywhere.

No switching houses to escape discipline.

No "good cop/bad cop."

If they lie to you Monday,

consequences next time you have them.   It doesn't have to be a full day, just for a short time.   Enough to let them know.

Your rules are portable.

Your leadership is portable.

Your authority is portable.

You are the **pillar**.

And pillars don't move.

Ive heard single parents say…I only get him/her/them on the weekends.   I cannot see myself grounding my child every time I have em..

It made me think.   When co parenting isn't available because the other parent actively undermines you, the discipline itself matters more

than your relationship.

Simply tell them "You don't have to like my rules but you do have to respect them" if they push, take the phone, iPad electronic for the night

(of course allowing the other parent to say his or her goodnights)

If you let things slide because of the limited time you have with the child/children, there will be pushback when you tighten up. So Stay steady.

The moment you fold because the child gets upset or because you feel bad, you reset the dynamic. They are testing authority, identity, and consistency.

Follow it up with " I love having fun and being with you, but fun doesn't cancel respect.

"I am you dad/mom first then I am your friend second. I can be fun and firm. Watch me"

THE SECRET THEY DON'T KNOW YOU KNOW

Strong-willed kids eventually soften around consistent parents. (I've seen it happen)

Manipulative kids stop manipulating around predictable parents.

Rebellious kids calm down around grounded parents.

The trick is not louder force it's quieter confidence.

A child can play two parents… but they cannot play a parent who cannot be moved.

You are unmovable.

You are unshakeable.

You are the anchor in their storm.

And even if they don't say it today

THEY KNOW IT.

AUTHORS NOTE

FINAL WORDS

Before you close this book, before life pulls you back into its noise, its chaos, its responsibilities, its routines…

let me speak to you one last time

not as an author,

not as a coach,

Or as a storyteller…

but as a mother.

As a woman who has survived storms most people never speak about.

As a daughter who had to raise herself.

As a woman who lost partners and buried pain,

As a woman who rebuilt life with her bare hands.

And as someone who learned the hard way that God's lessons often arrive in silence

before they arrive in miracles.

This book wasn't born from perfection. It was born from wounds that refused to rule me. From nights I cried quietly so my kids wouldn't hear.

From mornings I woke up with no strength except the kind God gives when He says, "Get up anyway."

I wrote this because I wished someone had written it for me.

I wrote this because I know what it feels like

to question every decision as a mother,

to carry guilt for things you didn't cause,

to break cycles you never asked to inherit,

to teach lessons you were never taught,

to feel alone even with a house full of people,

to hold the weight of "strong mother/father" when inside you feel anything but.

However, I also know what it feels like to witness growth in your children that you once prayed for, and still do.

To see them choose respect,

choose wisdom,

choose boundaries,

choose self-control,

choose faith and know deep down that your struggle was not in vain.

You might not get applause.

You might not get appreciation right away.

You might even be misunderstood in your own home.

But listen to me carefully:

You are shaping futures your children will one day thank you for even if they don't understand it today.

Your worth is not measured by your children's moods.

Your sacrifices are not invisible.

Your love is not forgotten.

Your efforts are not wasted.

Your discipline is not cruelty.

Your boundaries are not rejection.

Your consistency is not unnoticed.

You are raising adults who will one day navigate the world with the tools you placed in their hands and the strength you placed in their bones.   And if you're a teen reading this… hear me too:

Your mother is not against you.

She is not trying to control you or trying to limit you.

She is trying to save you from mistakes they've had to survive alone.   One day when life touches the same wounds she warned you about

you will hear her voice again and realize:

She wasn't lying. You just weren't ready to understand.

And this goes for the single dads too who are raising kids on their own

Mami nunca mintió. Tú nunca escuchaste.

But now? Now you do.

As you close this book, carry this truth:

Your future begins where your excuses end.

Your legacy begins where your self-control starts.

Your life begins again every time you choose discipline over comfort and healing over history.

And to you, mamá/papa the one reading this between responsibilities, between tears, between exhaustion and hope

I leave you with this blessing:

May God give you strength you didn't know existed.

May He give your children wisdom beyond their years.

May He protect your home with peace.

May He guide every decision you make.

May He reward every sacrifice you've ever made.

And may you remember every single day that you weren't chosen to be perfect.

You were chosen to be purposeful. And that, is more powerful than you will ever realize.

Con amor, con fuerza, y con fe (With love, strength and faith)

THE REBUTTAL
Before You Close This Book…

(For anyone who tries to rewrite my truth.)

Let's get one thing clear before you close these pages and go run your mouth with the wrong interpretation:

This last chapter was NOT a cry for pity. It was NOT a poetic diary. It was NOT a "feel bad for me, I survived so much."

No..

It was a *testimony*. A *blueprint*. A *weaponized prayer wrapped in paper*. A *battle cry written by a woman who bled, healed, and rose again.*

So let's correct these common lies **before they take root**:

MISREAD #1: "She's romanticizing struggle."

ABSOLUTELY NOT.

I'm exposing struggle so YOU don't drown in silence like I once did.

I'm turning pain into wisdom so my children and yours don't repeat the same cycles.

If you call that "romanticizing," it's because you've never transformed a wound into a weapon.

MISREAD #2: "She's making motherhood look dramatic."

First of all if you think motherhood **isn't** dramatic, you've either never raised kids or your kids raise YOU.

This chapter isn't dramatic. It's **accurate**. Real motherhood is spiritual warfare, emotional surgery,

and divine resilience at the same time. It takes a village

If you want a soft, pastel, influencer version of parenting… Instagram is free. This book ain't that.

MISREAD #3: "She's saying parents always know best."

No.

I'm saying parents who HEAL

and parents who GROW

parents who self-reflect

and parents who BREAK CYCLES know better than the children who are still *building*.

There's a difference.

I don't know everything.

But I sure know more than a teenager who thinks TikTok gurus are prophets.

MISREAD #4: "She's guilt-tripping kids."

ABSOLUTELY NOT.

I'm REVEALING how love WORKS.

A child who never feels discomfort grows into an adult who can't handle life.

A child who never hears hard truth grows into an adult who breaks under pressure.

If accountability feels like guilt to you, that says more about your upbringing than my writing.

MISREAD #5: "She's acting like all parents are perfect."

STOP.

I said the OPPOSITE.

I said we're wounded. We make mistakes. Some of us parent the way we wish someone parented us.

We fail, we cry, we overthink, we pray. This final chapter is honest because perfection never saved a child but authenticity always has.

MISREAD #6: "She's telling parents to abandon their kids to consequences."

Not abandonment… **alignment**.

I'm saying let LIFE teach the lesson while YOU provide the recovery.

That's not abandonment.

That's strategy.

That's neuroscience.

That's Biblical wisdom.

That's leadership.

MISREAD #7: "She's telling teens to just accept everything their parents say."

Incorrect.

I'm teaching teens how to recognize the difference between CONTROL and **PROTECTION**.

Between LIMITS and **LOVE**.

Between lectures and **lived experience**.

If it triggered you, you weren't listening your pride was.

MISREAD #8: "She's glorifying being a strong mother alone."

NO.

I'm glorifying **survival** when support never came.

I'm glorifying **faithfulness** when abandonment was the only inheritance.

I'm glorifying **God's covering** when the world turned its back.

This chapter isn't a celebration of single motherhood.

It's a celebration of the women who REFUSED to let single motherhood destroy them.

THE TRUTH YOU CAN'T IGNORE

This last page is not an ending. It's a mirror.

It shows you what parenting REALLY is:

Leadership

Legacy

Love that doesn't collapse

Discipline that doesn't break

Healing that doesn't hide

Faith that doesn't waver

Strength that doesn't beg for applause

If someone twisted it into anything else, that's because they read it with wounds, not wisdom.

COMMON MISUNDERSTANDINGS

Let's clear something up right now, antes que alguien abra la boca con opinión prestada de Facebook.

People LOVE to misunderstand parents like me especially when we raise our kids with backbone, boundaries, God, science, and strategy.

So here are the top misconceptions people like to whisper….   …and here are the TRUTHS that shut them down.

MISUNDERSTANDING #1: "She's not hard enough or too soft"

Last I checked, the world isn't handing out participation trophies for emotional fragility.

Softness without structure = chaos.

Comfort without discipline = incompetence.

Freedom without responsibility = disaster.

I don't raise kids to survive *my house*

I raise kids to survive the **real world**.

MISUNDERSTANDING #2: "She doesn't let her kids be kids."

Children ARE kids.   But that doesn't mean they need to grow up ignorant, dependent, or clueless.

In my house?

We play.

We joke.

We dance salsa in the kitchen.

We talk trash like a novela scene.

We pray.

We cry.

We laugh until our stomach hurts.

BUT we also build character. If that bothers you it's because nobody built yours.

MISUNDERSTANDING #3: "She thinks she's better than other parents."

ABSOLUTELY NOT.

I just refuse to settle for "barely surviving."

I don't think I'm better.

I think I'm **intentional**.

I teach my kids:

✓ control your emotions

✓ take responsibility

✓ communicate with respect

✓ choose people wisely

✓ handle business

✓ seek God

✓ use your brain

✓ build your future

✓ break cycles

If that looks like "better" to you, that's your insecurity talking, not my writing.

MISUNDERSTANDING #4: "She's too spiritual."

Mira…

I tried life WITHOUT God once.   It didn't work.

This book mixes neuroscience and faith because your brain and your spirit are not enemies.

They're teammates.   And if that offends you, take it up with the One who designed both.

This one always comes from people whose grown children STILL don't know how to fold a towel

or pay a bill

or apologize

or take rejection

or regulate their emotions

or choose a decent partner

or show up on time

or keep a promise

or stay consistent for longer than a week.

Or cook a meal

Produce helpless adults?

No, gracias.

I don't raise ornaments

I raise pillars.

MISUNDERSTANDING #6: "She's dramatic."

Of course. Duhhh

When a Latina mother speaks with passion, people call it "drama."

When a tired white father whispers softly, they call it "gentle parenting."

Be serious.   If a man said half the things I said in this book they'd publish it in a leadership manual

and charge $999 for a conference ticket.

I'm not dramatic.

I'm **authentically intense**.

I write in 4K emotion because parenting is lived in 4K emotion.

MISUNDERSTANDING #7: "She's too confident in her methods."

Listen…

I didn't write this book because I'm perfect.

I wrote it because I'm experienced.

I buried partners.

I raised babies into teens-future adults

I created a life out of ashes.

I parented myself while parenting them.

I prayed through storms.

I led a household with faith and strategy.

If I sound confident it's because I EARNED IT.

MISUNDERSTANDING #8: "This is too much for some parents."

GOOD.

This book isn't for parents who want comfort.

It's for parents who want transformation.

It's for parents who want to break curses.

It's for parents who want leaders, not liabilities.

It's for parents who know strength is beautiful but softness is NECESSARY.

If "too much" scares you, parenthood is gonna eat you alive.

THE ABSOLUTE TRUTH:

I don't raise kids so the world can approve of me.   I raise kids so GOD can be proud of me, so their FUTURE can be solid, and so my BLOODLINE never goes back to the pain I crawled out of.

You don't have to like my methods.

You don't have to agree with every chapter.

You don't have to raise kids like I do.

But don't misunderstand me.

My fire is not anger.

It's purpose.

My discipline is not cruelty.

It's preparation.

My tone is not aggression.

It's urgency.

My passion is not exaggeration.

It's conviction.

And my love?

My love is undefeated.

www.ingramcontent.com/pod-product-compliance
Lightning Source LLC
Chambersburg PA
CBHW041116300426
44111CB00003B/66